Contents

KW-325-262

To the memory of my parents

Acknowledgments

I am greatly indebted to Dr Freda Newcombe of the Neuropsychology Unit, The Churchill Hospital, Oxford, for encouragement and useful critical comment on the entire draft of this book, and also to Dr Richard West, Consultant Paediatrician at St George's Hospital, for advice on Chapters 1, 2 and 3.

To Lady Plowden I owe a special debt of gratitude, not only for reading the draft and commenting usefully, but also for writing the Foreword. Her enthusiasm and interest in the education of young children is undiminished despite her many other commitments.

I am grateful to Miss Hilda Archer for the pieces on play on pages 71, 94, to the authors of the books and papers which I have consulted and used in this book and to the many heads and class-teachers who have been generous with their observations and comments at courses. They have helped to root theory firmly in day-to-day practice and experience.

Dr W. R. Russell, former Professor of Neurology at Oxford has kindly read the proofs of this book but much more, has provided new insight for me into the links between brain studies and learning.

I would like to thank Mrs L. A. Morgan for her patience in typing the lectures on which this book is based. Finally I wish I could find a new way of expressing gratitude to Ann who has helped to clear up many errors of style and meaning. Needless to say any errors of fact and judgment are my own.

John Brierley
October 1977
Bristol

Foreword by Lady Plowden

Anyone who reads the newspapers regularly cannot fail to be aware that there is a great interest in and concern for the preschool child. This is reflected also both on television and on the radio. The discussion and debate, however, seem largely to centre on what should be provided either by the state or by voluntary organizations. There is a strong lobby for more nursery education, either in nursery schools or nursery classes. Under the 1944 Act, local authorities were 'to have regard for the need to provide' nursery education but, nevertheless, because of other priorities it is still only provided for about a third of the child population. It was the shortage of nursery education which was responsible for the spectacular growth of preschool playgroups. Starting in 1960 with the needs of one child, those belonging to the Preschool Playgroups Association now give companionship and opportunity for play to nearly 45,000 children. The needs of working mothers and of single parents for day nurseries have been stressed, particularly owing to the growth of both these categories. Recently there has been a growing realization of the role that is played by child minders; the inadequacy of this system has been recognized, with some constructive projects being devised to strengthen and improve the care which is given, by giving support to the minders themselves. The work of one service, however, seems to be rarely mentioned, either in the press or by the broadcasters; this is that of the Health Visitor, and yet to the majority of young mothers she must be in the early months of a child's life a well-known source of information, support and a ready help in trouble.

The emphasis of the publicity which is given seems to be on the 'preschool' child; this is popularly thought to mean the child in the two or three years before starting compulsory schooling at the age of five. Most mothers, with their child approaching this 'preschool age', will be aware of the choice of services available and know which they want for their child.

There seems, however, to be gaps in the information which is given by the media about the needs of preschool children. The first is crucial – that the preschool age does not begin only at two or three years old, but at birth and even before; the second, the important part that parents, and particularly a mother or mother-substitute, have to play in helping a child to develop all his faculties.

Many parents may absorb the fact that the interest of the mother and of the father is vital to the best development of the baby – that the baby must be talked to, played with and given suitable objects to use so that he may have a varied range of experiences. Parents may too easily feel that in knowing this, putting it into effect as far as they can, and that provided the child starts to walk and talk at what seem to be the appropriate moments, all is well. Further, they may feel that by sending the child for nursery education at the age of two or three they will have provided a sound educational start. By then it is too late. In addition, the parent who has not understood the needs of the developing baby may feel that her educational role is finished, that the educationists will take over and may herself opt out from further educational responsibility. Indeed, because the needs of all-round development of the young child have not been fully understood, complaints may follow that the child in his nursery schooling or his early years at school is being allowed to 'play' instead of getting down to what is thought of as real learning.

It is one thing to know that it is good to talk to a baby, that young children need sand and water with which to experiment, that touch and sound and sight and physical dexterity are important. It is however *why* this should be so which gives depth to this knowledge. Dr Brierley, in terms which a layman can understand, has added this depth in his explanation of the intricate construction and functioning of the brain and of its relationship with the development of all a child's abilities.

Much of what he writes will strike mothers as something that they may well feel they have known all along. As long ago as 1918 Margaret McMillan wrote of her nursery, 'We shall try like the unwearying sea to win at last a new and higher conception of home as a place that must include nurseries, talks around the fire, stories, games, music and something more that makes all these shine as memories for evermore.' The games our grandmothers played with us as very small children were of educational value, developing the sense of sound and touch and sight and thought.

But parents today have lost confidence in themselves as parents and with any encouragement are willing to hand over responsibility to the professionals. This is not from lack of interest in their children but from lack of confidence in themselves as parents. This lack of confidence springs, I believe, from lack of knowledge of the why and wherefore of what they may feel instinctively that they should do. The knowledge to back it up is too often lacking.

With smaller families, with more labour-saving devices, I hope that many parents will have time to study the remarkable and complicated make-up of their baby, so that they may regain from this knowledge their confidence as parents. In so doing, they may understand that there is no rule of thumb to be applied blindly and incomprehendingly but a gradation of emphases which must be tailored to meet the needs of a very small individual who has to grow up capable of living in an increasingly changing world.

BHP
1st September 1977

Introduction

This book is mainly for the parents of young children but it may be useful for others professionally concerned with children at this stage of development. In it I have said something about health care and growth because physical and mental health go hand in hand, but the main theme is the care of the young brain and intellect. Comfortingly, much of what brain studies have told us confirms commonsense and what we know in our bones already.

Children spend a surprisingly small proportion of their waking time at school; only 4 per cent of the first five years for a child who attends morning nursery school between three and five years. From five to sixteen years, when school is compulsory, the figure rises only to 17 per cent. All the same, after the parents the teacher has perhaps the most influence on the child and it is important that parents and teachers should try to work together. Parents need to understand why the brain's capabilities can be hampered by 'shut-up' answers and by clamping down on exploratory play. Just as the wrong food will rot the teeth, so lack of stimulus will lead to a creeping decay of the mind. If disadvantage follows disadvantage in a relentless train right through childhood, then a caries of the mind develops that no amount of later effort will remove. The odds are heavily against some children as the following example shows. A mother brought her three and a half year old to a nursery school. The child could only say two words, 'tea' and 'please'. When his mother was tackled about this she replied, 'He doesn't talk, he has only just come to school.' She thought it was the school's job to teach him to speak. This is an extreme example (and of course the child may have been abnormal) but it is the kind of disadvantage which throws a long shadow forward. There are too many homes that to quote Professor Hawkins (1977):

. . . are merely shells, devoid of affection, of maturity, of unselfishness, empty of any routine or planning.

There are no routines or times for getting up, or going to bed. Meal times do not exist. Meals are not even served on a table. Meal-time chat is unknown. Food is grabbed from a shelf, from a cornflake packet or a tin in the intervals between TV programmes.

Children wander in and out of these empty unfurnished caves as the adults themselves do, without any purpose or pattern in their lives. In these vacuum homes a generation of our children – half our future – is learning to become in its turn a generation of inadequate parents in a never-ending vicious circle.

In plain language, the child who gets most from home gets most from school.

There are three special marks of mankind: his long childhood; his flexible, open mind (a mind which makes us aware of many-sided connections between us and the world around us, between the past and the future and between that we can actually observe and that which is more intuitive); and his individuality. All three call for definite strategies in teaching and learning.

Man's long childhood – the twelve or thirteen years before the adolescent growth spurt changes a child into a young adult (and especially the first five years of a child's life) – is a crucially important time for physical and intellectual development. Severe physical or emotional or intellectual deprivation during this time can cripple the child and therefore the adult. In this book I have tried to identify the physical and intellectual needs of the young child and to suggest ways of meeting them. I have also tried to explain the whys behind some of the traditional 'do's and don'ts' parental commonsense has established.

I hope that *Growing and Learning* will help all those concerned with young children – health visitors, nursery nurses, playgroup leaders and of course parents and teachers – to work together to make sure that every child can realize his unique potential.

Reference
HAWKINS, E. (1977) Speech given to the Association of Headmistresses Conference

Chapter 1

The vulnerable brain

In rich countries like Britain you rarely see a scraggy, poor-looking child running the streets. We have come some way from the 'utterly neglected and hopeless' life and time of Charles Dickens, or from Charlotte Brontë's Lowood where the Sunday treat was a 'double ration of bread – a whole instead of a half slice – with the delicious addition of a thin scrape of butter'. No exaggeration for the times, this.

Infant mortality

In contrast to the gloomy, austere picture of not so long ago, most children today are healthier than ever before. Better food and social conditions and the conquest of infectious diseases like whooping cough, measles, diphtheria, and scarlet fever, which were killers in the past century, mean that children are taller and heavier and that fewer of them die than at any previous time. The death rate for infants under one, commonly called the infant mortality rate, is a sensitive barometer of lifestyle, with a high rate marking persistent underprivilege. It is now about 14 per 1,000 live births in England. At the turn of the century it was 150; in 1911 it was 130, and even in 1931 it was 66. Grossly bad conditions do still exist however and the last chapter of this book shows that they are still related to the infant mortality rate. There are black spots even now. In Lambeth, for instance, the rate is 21 per 1,000, but a few miles away and a few steps up the social scale in Bromley it is 12. In Bradford it is 25; Tameside 29, but in Oxfordshire only 13. But while infant mortality rates have declined dramatically in England and Wales, we still lag behind other countries, lying eleventh out of seventeen for infant mortality and ninth for perinatal mortality (stillbirths and deaths under one week).

Infant mortality is a finely balanced gauge which sums up general living conditions in one figure. Overcrowding, bad housing, ignorant mothers who do not bother to keep their antenatal appointments, lack of a proper place to store food leading to food poisoning and gastroenteritis, are all drawn together in the index of infant mortality. It throws a spotlight on general living standards which, in turn, affect the growth and development of children.

We are all aware that bad conditions can damage physical health and kill babies. It is not so obvious that they may also affect the developing brain and leave a mark on the intellect.

Early brain development

The human brain develops faster than the rest of the body. At birth it is about 25 per cent of its adult weight; at six months nearly 50 per cent; at two and a half years about 75 per cent; at five nearly 90 per cent; and at ten it is 95 per cent grown (see Table 1 below). The big spurt in brain growth starts in the womb towards the end of the first six months of pregnancy and slows at around two years. There is a smaller spurt earlier on from the twelfth to the eighteenth week of pregnancy. This represents the multiplication of nerve cells and

Table 1 The growth of the human brain

Age	Weight of brain (in grams)
Newborn	340
6 months	750
1 year	970
2 years	1,150
3 years	1,200
6 years	1,250
9 years	1,300
12 years	1,350
20 years	1,400

The rate of growth is highest before birth but notice that the weight nearly triples during the first year of life. Good nutrition is crucial during this early growth spurt.

probably happens at a time when the baby is well protected from external influences. The major growth spurt reflects growth and branching of nerve cells with no increase in their number and marks a sensitive time for the brain.

I have stressed increase in the *quantity* of brain but of course this may not be the heart of the matter. What may be more important in the development of the brain's capabilities is its *internal* organization and in particular the branching of the nerve cells.

The food requirements of the fast growing brain before birth, and in the first two or three years of life are great. Just before birth and in the first year of life the baby's brain needs large quantities of protein from meat, eggs and milk, and astonishingly grows at the rate of one to two milligrammes every minute. Hand in hand with the physical growth of the brain the intellect is developing fast.

The growth spurts of the brain

During the major growth spurt of the brain, starting towards the last six months of pregnancy and ending at about two, important changes are taking place in the brain cortex, the grey matter of the brain which helps us to think. The billions of nerve cells there are growing and branching to form dense webs of connections. The parts of the nerve cells that connect (at nerve 'synapses') are the fine tendrils called the dendrites. Under the microscope a slice of brain tissue from the grey matter of a child of six looks like a dense forest of tree branches (see Figure 1, page 16). At birth there are only a few branches. There must be rapid sprouting of the nerve cells and the formation of rich interconnections from birth onwards. Research carried out on rats shows that malnourishment causes them not only to have lighter brains but also causes a big (40 per cent) reduction in the connections made at nerve synapses. It is thought, but not yet established, that the richness of branching and connecting of the nerves in the grey matter is important in the development of intelligence. Certainly the starved rats were clumsier than normally-fed rats.

For man the major growth spurt of the brain, lasting for about twenty-seven to twenty-eight months, may be a time when the brain has a 'once only' opportunity to grow properly. During this time the baby is staring, watching mother, feeling, tasting, listening – in short exploring his world. If the brain is starved of food now, the dendrites may not branch out properly and the intellect may be lowered. Even a tiny reduction in branching (beyond the range of our present techniques of measurement) may lower the capabilities of the brain. And the consequences could be permanent.

Figure 1 Nerve cells in the grey matter of a child at birth (A) and of another at six (B)

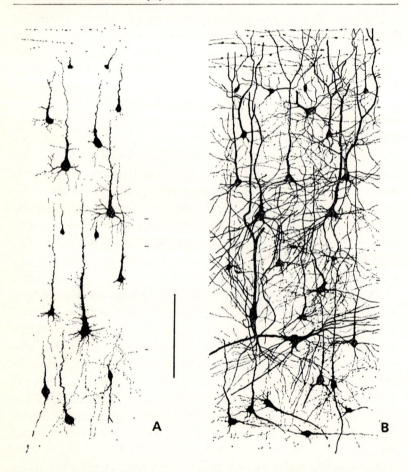

The scale (line) represents 120μm. (From Conel, J. Le R. (1939–67) *The Postnatal Development of the Human Cerebral Cortex* (eight volumes) Harvard.)

Malnutrition and brain development

There are a few important questions to ask and to try to answer about brain development. Can bad feeding hurt the brain and the intellect? Are there vulnerable times in the development of the brain when poor food might have especially serious consequences? Are there optimum times for learning when the brain is unusually sensitive? If there are, and these sensitive periods are neglected, the best time for acquiring a skill may pass and it will never be learned so easily again. In the same way birds learn to sing and fly rapidly at the right stage but these activities are impaired if the crucial period is missed.

Malnutrition cannot easily be separated from poverty in general. It is but one part of a dark cloud which hangs over many families and may not be so harmful in damping the intellect as lack of talk and play. Poor diet and lack of play and language are part of the impoverished syndrome and their combined effect on mental development in the young can be as grave as physical battering.

Not surprisingly the effects of chronic malnutrition in the child vary according to his age (see Table 2, page 18). If it occurs throughout pregnancy, as in many mothers in South America, India and Africa, the baby may have a lower birth weight and smaller brain than average. Such a child could be backward. *Short* periods of malnutrition during pregnancy and in the early years do not seem to have a lasting effect on the intellect.

Chronic malnutrition before two or three years of age, especially shortage of protein and of the vitamins and minerals necessary for growth, does seem to cause lowered IQ. Physically too the brain suffers from malnutrition. Children in South America who died of malnutrition had fewer brain cells than children who had died from other causes. Timing seems to be of critical importance. Chronic undernutrition happening for the first time in children older than three years seems to have no lasting effects. Even as late as two, better protein feeding can improve IQ by as much as eighteen points but only, of course, in a specially selected group of children that have been seriously undernourished. I doubt whether more meat, milk or eggs would have any significant effect on a normally-fed child.

All these findings were from countries where extreme undernutrition is not uncommon. Serious deprivation of food is probably

Table 2 Diets of five-year-old children

United Kingdom		S. and E. India	
Breakfast		Rice	6 oz (170 g)
Cornflakes	½ oz (14 g)	Brown sugar	2 oz (57 g)
Milk	5 oz (140 g)	Dried fish	½ oz (14 g)
Bread	1 oz (28 g)	Vegetables	
Butter	½ oz (14 g)	**Total**	
Bacon	1 oz (28 g)	**kilocalories**	**900**
Tomato	2 oz (57 g)	**protein**	**25 g**
Midmorning			
orange juice	5 oz (140 g)		
Dinner		*Ghana, village near Kumasi*	
Steak	2 oz (57 g)	Plantain	2½ oz (70 g)
Carrots	2 oz (57 g)	Cocoyam	8 oz (230 g)
Potatoes	2 oz (57 g)	Cassava	1½ oz (42 g)
Milk pudding	5 oz (140 g)	Beans and nuts	⅕ oz (5 g)
Tea		Cocoyam leaf	½ oz (14 g)
Egg	2 oz (57 g)	Fish and meat	⅓ oz (10 g)
Bread	2 oz (57 g)	Red palm oil	
Butter	¾ oz (20 g)	Egg plant	
Jam	½ oz (14 g)	Red peppers	
Apple	4 oz (114 g)	Onions	
Milk	5 oz (140 ml)	**Total**	
Bedtime		**kilocalories**	**430**
Milk	5 oz (140 ml)	**protein**	**11 g**
Total			
kilocalories	**1,500**		
protein	**60 g**		

These are of course average figures which conceal a great deal of variation but the facts speak for themselves. The poor diet in both Ghana and India does not provide sufficient energy (nor protein in the Ghana village) for a five year old. Broadly speaking lack of animal food means a lack of good quality protein. (From P. Fisher and A. Bender (1970) *The Value of Food* Oxford University Press.)

quite rare in these islands now, though I think we have to be cautious about this. There are many children in this and other rich countries who are born much too early and in whom the steep part of the brain growth will be postnatal. Thus the feeding of the prematurely born may be highly significant for proper brain development. Also a significant number of British babies are born with a low birth weight, though not prematurely. They are victims of slow growth in the womb at the very time which is crucial for brain building.

Good nutrition is vital in the mother in the foetal and suckling stages and in the child at least until the age of two.

Smoking, drinking and the brain

As well as malnutrition, smoking and alcohol can affect the brain of the unborn child. A mother who smokes regularly during pregnancy runs the risk of having a child low in birth weight, shorter than average, backward in general intelligence and behind in reading. To be precise, at eleven years children whose mothers smoked were on average three months behind other children in general intelligence, backward by four months in reading (possibly smoking during pregnancy reduces the number of cells in the baby's brain) and one centimetre shorter in height. These were the lucky children. Something like 1,500 babies die in Britain every year as a result of their mothers smoking and others may be permanently disabled by cerebral palsy. The message is this: if a mother wants a healthy child she must not smoke during the whole nine months of pregnancy. Nor should husbands smoke for their smoke may be passed on to the baby from a smoke-filled room. The babies die because smoking produces smaller babies who have more chance of being stillborn or dying in the first week of life.

Alcohol in *excess* is bad. Indeed, a link has been established between excessive drinking and poor growth in a baby, small head and mental retardation. So a mother should avoid heavy spirits and stick to lighter beers and wines.

I have talked about the brain and its vulnerability to poor feeding at an early stage and to the sensitivity of the unborn child's brain to smoking, chronic malnutrition and alcohol in excess. What about its sensitivity to other effects of the environment: to adequate stimulus through talk and play?

Sensitive periods

We know from animal experiments that the nervous system is most impressionable to the effects of the environment during periods of rapid growth and development, such as occur in the human brain when it is growing rapidly after birth and in the first few years of life. We do not know much about sensitive periods though clear evidence is emerging from some animal experiments that they do exist. We need to note these animal experiments in relation to learning because the implications of such facts for us are important. To illustrate their relevance I want to describe briefly some important work on brain plasticity in cats, though similar results have been obtained in other animals.

As I have just stressed, the nerve-cell connections in the brain are changing and developing in early childhood and the richness of branching may be related to ability. In man this nerve development may well continue into adult life because man's slow development gives him a plasticity and resilience not found in animals with their quicker development. In animals however the nerve connections seem to *fix* after a certain critical time, making them far less plastic to the effects of the environment.

If one eye of an *adult* cat is covered with an opaque substance that lets in light but not pattern, there is no change in the behaviour or electrical activity of the brain cells after three months. Pattern can be distinguished. The cat is quite normal. Kittens, on the other hand, seem to be totally blind in the eye that has been covered for three months. The eye is normal. It is the brain which is affected; the nerve pathways appear to have degenerated through 'lack of experience'.

But we can be more precise about timing. Other experiments with cats show that the period of high sensitivity starts suddenly at about twenty-one days after birth, reaching peak sensitivity during the fourth, fifth and sixth weeks, and declining gradually until about the fourteenth week. During the time of acute sensitivity, on the twenty-eighth day of life, only one hour of exposure to a certain pattern is enough to tune every brain cell in the seeing area of the brain to that particular pattern.

While we do not know for certain what happens physically in the human brain, there are a few bits and pieces of evidence which show that the young brain is impressionable to the environment. Indeed it is very likely that periods of maximum sensitivity to learning occur in children rather than of critical 'now or neverness'. Here are four pieces of evidence which show that the human brain might have periods of sensitivity.

1   In children it is well known that squint can permanently impair vision if it is not corrected in early childhood. Most squints arise between two and four years of age, and research has shown that the brain is vulnerable to the effects of abnormal vision before about the age of three. Squint affects vision because, if uncorrected, it results in the failure of the child and the future adult to develop full binocular vision with depth perception, i.e. to appreciate objects in 3D. Depth perception depends on the proper nerve-cell connections forming to link brain cells fed by one eye with those fed by another. They have got to be in balance. By three they are formed and damage to vision after three years can be irreversible if squint is not corrected.

2   In the treatment of lazy eye, the good eye has a patch over it. If the lazy eye is not treated and made to work it can become almost completely functionless through lack of use by failure of this eye to make proper nerve connections with the seeing parts of the brain.

3   There is a piece of evidence that the type of visual environment a child is brought up in affects the tuning of the brain cells concerned with vision. The Cree Indians live in wigwams and are unused to the horizontal/vertical lines of modern Western architecture. They cannot pick out in tests horizontal and vertical lines as well as oblique ones. But children who grow up in Western countries are better at recognizing horizontal/vertical patterns.

4   The child has an optimum time when his developing brain can master the skill of talking. After about twelve a child suffering bad brain damage on the left side may not be able to speak, but in cases of early damage to the left side of the head, a new speech area is set up in the opposite side of the brain. The young brain is very flexible.

This evidence then does seem to show that early experience is crucial to animals and perhaps to us in the development of the brain's capabilities. Early in life it seems as if the brain's nerve connections are susceptible and become tuned to the influence of the environment.

The picture as presented above is pretty depressing and points to the crucial quality of early experience influencing the brain. The vital question is: is a bad start irreversible? We need more evidence, one way or the other. James Kagan (1974), Professor of Child Development at Harvard, has produced some strange but fascinating evidence that, even after a bad start, the human brain can catch up, given proper stimulation, a point which is of enormous importance to foster and adoptive parents.

Children in certain Indian villages of Guatemala are kept in dark huts and are hardly spoken to or played with for most of the first year of their lives, although they are loved by their parents. After twelve to eighteen months the greatly retarded children leave their huts and are allowed to explore. By the age of ten their retardation has faded and they are gay, alert and intellectually competent children.

From this Professor Kagan concludes that the human brain does seem to have the capacity to catch up after a bad start. But if a child, after a poor start, continues to grow up in poor, unstimulating surroundings, if his bad experiences are cumulative, I doubt whether there is much hope of his ever catching up.

Birth to twelve: the crucial years for learning

It is possible that the period of great sensitivity to the environment coincides not only with the big spurt in brain growth up to the age of five, but continues during the years right up to puberty, twelve to thirteen, when the senses are sharp and the brain is in a formative state. This idea is supported by children's physical growth pattern, which is an evolutionary adaptation to the learning situation (see Figure 2, opposite).

Up to puberty, children, unlike other animals, are adapted to pass through a long period when they are relatively small and weak. During this time they can be kept in order and taught and can play with others without hurting themselves too much. At puberty the growth spurt turns children into adults, themselves capable of dominating the young and looking after them. Rapid learning, absorbing experience through the senses, language, play, exploration and through imitation of adults, is a factor of the early years from birth to twelve. These are perhaps the crucial years which evolution has timetabled as the years of very rapid learning and brain development and relatively slow body growth.

Figure 2 Graphs showing the growth of tissues and parts of the body as a percentage of the total gain from birth to twenty

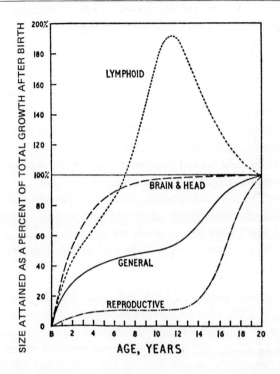

At aged five the brain is about 90 per cent grown, the body about 40 per cent, the reproductive organs 10 per cent and the lymphoid tissue (certain glands like the thymus and also the lymph nodes) 80 per cent (though at the age of eleven it reaches almost double its eventual size). The lymphoid tissue curve is quite different from the others; it develops early as a defence against infections because the baby and infant freshly exposed to a new world is then actively acquiring immunity. The tissue thus reaches a maximum value by the start of adolescence, then decreases. Sometimes children have troublesomely large (but normal) tonsils and adenoids but generally can be expected to lose snorts and snuffles when adolescence starts. Notice how the reproductive organs develop late, not until the development of the brain and head have ceased. Note that it is not only the brain that develops early but also the skull, eyes and ears.

Thus the timetabling of different parts of the body appears to be geared for learning early: a child is small, can be controlled, his brain and sense organs are developed and he is sexually immature. (After J. M. Tanner (1972) *Education and Physical Growth* University of London Press.)

We have seen that good nutrition and proper stimulus are vital to the development of the intellect of the baby and growing child. What then are the true indicators of deprivation? Fear and cruelty, poor talk, lack of sensory experience through not having lots of things to touch, smell and look at, few books and toys, and clamping down on children's natural exploratory activities, may permanently retard mental development, not necessarily by altering nerve pathways, though this is quite possible, but by creating an unsatisfactory state of mind by poor motivation and by learning to expect little out of life. The Court Report lends weight to what I have said. We have a duty to intervene where children are crippled by circumstance. To quote the Report (DHSS 1977):

. . . the disadvantages of birth and early life cast long shadows forward. . . . We now know that the effects of early disadvantage can be much diluted by the environmental circumstances the child encounters during the middle and later years of childhood; and that it is especially worth making this corrective effort because early disadvantage tends to lead to later disadvantage, so that unless there is intervention there develops a compounding of difficulties. It is this train of events which is influential rather than the critical effect of particular circumstances in early life considered in their own right.

The human brain is robust and can catch up after inadequate intellectual stimulation in infancy but the early years are nonetheless much more significant for later development than was realized until recently.

References

DHSS (1977) *Fit for the Future* (The Court Report) HMSO
KAGAN, J. (1974) Man's enormous capacity to catch up *Times Educational Supplement* September

Chapter 2

Growing and developing

Another sensitive measure of child health is growth in height. Like infant mortality we consider this subject in relation to averages of groups of children rather than individuals in whom allowances have to be made for hereditary differences. We can, for instance, look for average differences in height between occupational classes – the 'social classes' of the Registrar General known as: I professional; II intermediate; III skilled; IV partly skilled; V unskilled. The relevance of such measures is that average differences, some of them surprising, can be seen between different groups, and as a result specific questions can be asked about their possible causes and how these may be compensated for. Then, if society wishes, programmes can be devised that try to compensate for, say, a special group handicap like backwardness in reading.

Growth in height: a sensitive measure of health
Growth in height is a good measure of the health of children because as Professor Tanner, an expert on child development, has pointed out, growth integrates all the tiny influences playing on a child year by year. It is 'incredibly sensitive, yet solidly permanent,' Tanner (1976) says 'and it can be measured objectively.' I shall return to these influences presently but let us look now at some details of growth.

Growth before birth
In a baby the fastest growth in length is *before* birth at about four months from conception when growth is taking place at a rate of ten to twelve centimetres each month. Before this growth is slow and afterwards declines. Never again does a child grow so fast.

Growth in weight follows the same general pattern but the fastest weight gain is approximately two months *after* birth, and then there is a slowing in rate. From about thirty-six weeks to birth at forty weeks, the baby slows down in rate of growth and this may be the effect of space in the womb. Twins slow down sooner when their combined weight is equal to that of a thirty-six-week-old single baby. If a child's hereditary blueprint is bigness, the slowing-down mechanism helps such a child to be born easily to a small woman. In fact the particularly big child has an inheritance which makes itself felt only after birth and thus given the right conditions for growth, a baby born small grows fast in the first three years and again in adolescence under the guidance of heredity. A major factor in birth weight is the birth weight of the mother; mothers of small babies were often themselves small at birth.

At birth boys weigh on average about 3 kilograms, girls slightly less. The average length of boys and girls at birth is around 50 centimetres.

Growth after birth

Growth in height is an increase in the distance from the top of the head to the heels. The speed or 'velocity' of this growth is the increase in distance over a certain period of time, mainly measured in centimetres per year. Velocity or rate is used in exactly the same way as when talking about the speed of cars in miles per hour. Just as a car may speed up or slow down within an hour, so the speed of growth may change from one part of a year to another, but this is not to say that growth takes place in fits and starts, it is a smooth process.

At birth a child is growing faster than at any other time in life but not as fast as before birth. But the speed of growth in height declines from birth onwards, and it is in early childhood that the drop in the speed of growth is most dramatic. It then declines very slowly and from about the age of six until puberty is reached, growth in height is nearly constant year by year. Then, quite suddenly during the adolescent spurt, the slow rate is reversed and there is a dramatic acceleration. For a year or two the child shoots up, growing at the rate of when he was two or three. After this burst, speed of growth declines, becomes progressively slower, and stops.

This description is a coarse one and there are finer periods of growth which underline the general growth rate. Within a year's space, as parents must have noticed, children of between five and nine do not grow at the same speed. For some the slowest growth takes place between August and December, the fastest between January and July. For others there are comparable changes in growth rate but apparently independent of season. Before about five, when the speed of growth is decelerating rapidly, and during the adolescent spurt, seasonal changes in growth rate are masked by the speed of the overall change. Growth in weight is fastest in the autumn.

There is some slight evidence that day length, which varies during the seasons, may affect growth, perhaps by influencing the glands controlling growth through the eyes. In totally blind children the rate of growth does not vary much with the seasons as it does with children of normal sight. Blind children do not grow at a constant rate but their fastest and slowest growth may take place in any season.

Puberty in boys and girls
The chief characteristics of the changes at puberty in boys are the development of the reproductive organs accompanied by the growth spurt, an increase in the size of muscles and in the limbs a loss of fat, and an increase in shape; the shoulders widen more than the hips, and there are changes in the shape of the face, lower jaw, and in the thickness of the neck. The voice becomes deeper due to the growth of the larynx. Pubic hair grows, followed by axillary and facial hair. In boys these changes can take place between nine and fifteen, with the peak growth rate on average at fourteen. These changes happen at different ages in different boys and the sequence in which they take place varies from one to another. Some pass through the whole sequence quickly, some slowly. It is interesting that although most of the skeleton takes part in the growth spurt, different parts grow at different times. Any mother will have noticed that boys go on outgrowing their jackets after they have stopped outgrowing their trousers. This is because the legs grow first, followed a few months later by broadening of the body, and a year or so later by increase in trunk length. Boys' big hands and feet accentuate their awkwardness. Hands and feet are the first part of the body to reach adult size but the rest of the body still has a long way to grow.

In girls the main changes at puberty are development of the breasts and pubic hair, the growth spurt, the onset of menstruation and eventually the attainment of fertility. As in boys there is a good deal of variation in the timing and sequence of these events. In general these changes take place between the ages of ten and fifteen with a peak growth rate at twelve on average and the first menstrual period taking place about a year after the peak height velocity has been reached. As in boys the growth spurt is accompanied by muscle growth but this is not as great as in boys and while boys lose fat during the growth spurt, girls do not.

Although the growth spurt happens earlier in girls than boys by about two years, other aspects of sexual development do not take place much later in boys than girls. Boys' reproductive organs start to develop about the same time as breasts in girls and complete sexual maturity is reached at about the same average age in both sexes. Girls' looks at puberty – bigger than boys with obvious breast development – make boys look immature. But in boys the early development of the reproductive organs is concealed by clothes, and the obvious changes – the shooting up in height, deepening of the voice and the development of facial hair – do not happen until the reproductive organs are nearly mature.

The age of menarche, or the first menstrual period, is one example of the wide variation in developmental age found in girls. On average this is just over aged thirteen but the normal range for 95 per cent of girls is from eleven to fifteen. The extreme range, taking in 99 per cent of girls, is from ten to sixteen.

Although differences in growth patterns exist between girls and boys, considerable variation is found among boys and among girls. Let us take two simple cases at the extremes: a child who is very tall and one who is very small.

Tall and short children
A boy (or girl) who is very tall compared with his friends, or parents who themselves are very tall and who are worried because they think they may have an exceptionally tall child, sometimes seek medical advice. Most of the children are, fortunately, perfectly normal and well, but girls may still be worried for social reasons. Predictions of future height, which has a big inherited component, can be made to

within three or four centimetres by X-ray of the wrist bones. Much more often than treatment, reassurance is necessary by doctors, teachers and parents, that a tall child will not end up a giant. Tall girls especially tend to slouch and they should be encouraged to hold themselves straight. There is a growing tendency in the medical profession to arrest the growth of girls who are predicted to reach adult heights which are socially unacceptable – 1·75 metres plus. This is done by giving hormones (oestrogens) to induce an early puberty and stop growth when the girl has reached a socially acceptable adult height.

Sometimes a child is tiny and parents are anxious to find out whether his growth is normal or not. Perhaps the parents are tall, or the boy or girl is the smallest in the class, or a younger child in the family is bigger, or he is not growing out of his clothes like other boys. A doctor should always be seen if the child fails to gain height so that proper treatment can be obtained if necessary.

Apart from some abnormalities, growth rates can be hampered by bad feeding, disease and unhappiness and return to normal height is accompanied by a big catch-up growth. How this catch-up growth works is not understood but its machinery is so sensitive and effective that it allows growth to return almost completely to its previous pattern after a setback.

Happiness, as we all know, is essential to good health and growth in children but it is hard to pin down as a very definite contributor to good health. Commonsense tells us that good food, warmth, comfort, cleanliness, love and a sympathetic ear are all important to health and growth and 'good' homes are not necessarily linked up with plenty of money. There is one classical case which 'proves' that good growth is linked with love and happiness. It happened in Germany in two orphanages just after the last war. Extra food was given to the children but it did not result in the expected growth. This was because it was given by a disagreeable, harsh and repressive sister-in-charge, who frightened the children. Only her favourites benefited from the extra food by gain in weight.

There is some evidence too that children do not grow so well in term-time as in school holidays, no matter whether they are day pupils or at boarding school. The effect of stress on happiness, appetite and consequently nutrition and growth is clearly complex, certainly involves the body glands and needs further investigation. But stress is known to cause wasting of muscle and other tissues, the muscle being turned into sugar for energy purposes.

The influence of family life

I said earlier that child growth is as finely balanced to family life as to outside influences. Family life, as we all know, has its ups and downs and although the mother has most contact with, and influence on, the children, the father's position is central. In a way he is like the sun. If he shines warmly, it gives a glow to a family. If he is overcast with bad moods and short-tempered after a bad day at work, then this reflects on the family and their health. It is one of the subtle influences mentioned by Professor Tanner (1976) that plays on and influences growth.

The family is under fire from some quarters these days but we have to remember that it is the product of thousands of years of evolution and must have survival value for man as a species. The family serves as a secure base from which a child can explore and test out the environment. It picks up the bits in times of stress and distress. And, most important, it sets a standard for the child so that he can establish his own. If talk is restricted and stifled by rows, bad moods and extremes of dominance or submission in the family, child health and growth become disordered.

Many children are brought up by single or divorced parents. Perhaps the bad effects of separation on the child have been over-stressed in the past. Where break-up of the marriage or partnership is preceded by prolonged discord, the behaviour of a child can be adversely affected; less so where a parent is lost through death. In plain terms family discord may be more damaging to a child than separation.

I mention these matters because it is easy to think only of good food as being essential for good growth. Not so; the Bible sums up human wisdom on this matter, 'better a dinner of herbs where love is, than a stalled ox and hatred therewith.'

Food and growth

Everyone will agree about the growing child's need for food both before and after birth and will probably be aware that this should be found in a good mixed diet. Closer examination shows just why the diet should be balanced, how it should vary for children of different ages, and the importance of some of its constituents to the growing body and brain.

Protein

In this country it is virtually impossible to eat too little or the wrong sort of protein in the diet because of the variety of foods available, but a few facts about protein foods will be helpful.

Protein is necessary in the diet for the body to make new protein for itself as it grows. Proteins are made up of long chains of amino acids linked together in complicated ways. The exact nature of a particular protein depends on which of the amino acids it consists of, how many amino acid units it contains and how they are linked together. Nine of these essential amino acids which are needed to make protein cannot be made by the body itself and must therefore be taken in through food. Some protein foods are short of one or two of these key acids but other foods contain them. The well-balanced diet will consist of foods which together contain all these acids in the right proportions. For instance, cornflakes alone do not contain all nine, but with added milk the balance is achieved. Jamaicans eat rice and peas to achieve the balance quite naturally and not with studied forethought. This adding together the right foods so the body can use them only works when the foods which make up the balance are eaten together or within an hour or two of each other. This not only achieves the magic combination of nine amino acids which can then make protein but the carbohydrate food also helps the absorption of protein. The very young brain and body are particularly hungry for protein and if a baby is to obtain the correct mix of amino acids in his diet, breast feeding is best. It is the most effective way of stopping undernutrition and supplying adequate protein. Babies have been fashioned to live on human milk and the mixtures of foods it contains are right. Mother's milk has the added bonus of protecting the child from certain diseases like gastroenteritis during the first vulnerable months of life because the milk contains antibodies before the baby develops his own. The simple message is to keep the feeding during the early months as natural as possible. Not only is milk the right fuel for the developing brain but it also helps to ward off disease.

There is an old tale that children require *much* more protein in their diet than adults. This is not necessarily so but, and it is a very big but, the proportion of the nine essential amino acids needs to be higher for children. For an adult virtually any protein will do, but a child, and more so an infant, needs foods high in these key amino acids, contained in milk, egg and meat (see Table 2, page 18). If these foods are not obtainable, he needs a higher proportion than an adult of lower quality protein, usually plant protein – grains, beans, cereals, vegetables. Most cultures seem to have natural food combinations which mix poor quality protein inadequate in certain essential amino acids with other protein acids containing foods which have balancing strengths and weaknesses. The resulting mixture provides all the nine amino acids essential for growth.

How much protein?

Not much protein is necessary for generally healthy populations. Most of the protein necessary for growth and repair of the body is obtained from the breakdown of protein that is already part of the body tissue. The body is like a very efficient chemical factory; there is little waste so that about 75 per cent of the amino acids used for growth and repair come from the breakdown of worn-out tissues already part of the body. Thus the daily amount of extra protein in the diet necessary for good health is small – about 30–35 grams on average from about the age of ten onwards. A little more is needed for boys and for pregnant mothers, and much more (45 grams) for nursing mothers. Roughly speaking, for normal purposes this means about 30 grams of protein a day in meat, fish, cheese, milk or eggs. For babies and children up to the age of nine, 15–25 grams is adequate (see Figure 3, page 33). This is not much when you think of all the protein we eat now: the diet of a huntsman rather than a city dweller. The wartime rations of thirty-five years ago (see Table 3, page 39) seem meagre, but perhaps made us healthier than we are now. Food was not so rich and we had enough protein.

Calories

Up to the age of one a child needs 1,000 Kcals of energy per day for growing and living (see Figure 3, page 33). This rises to 2,000 Kcals by the time he is six, as much as his mother but rather less than his

Figure 3 Recommended daily allowances for energy and protein (hatched bar graph, male; solid, female)

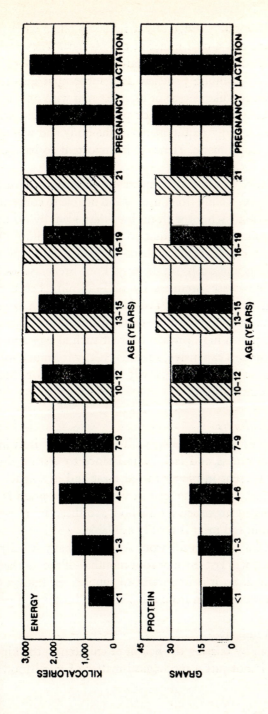

Requirements vary greatly with age and sex. Pregnancy and lactation increase nutritional need. Remember that recommended allowances are not absolute for individuals and can be justifiably applied only to reasonably healthy populations and may well be subject to revision as knowledge advances. (From N. S. Scrimshaw and V. S. Young (1977) The requirements of human nutrition *Scientific American*.)

father who needs about 3,000 Kcals if he is an office worker but more of course if he is a coal miner at the pit face. These calories come from carbohydrates (sugar and starch) and fats in the diet but also from the body-building proteins. If a substantial quantity of expensive protein food like cheese or meat is eaten with only a small quantity of starch-containing bread or potato, the protein will be wasted to meet the energy requirements of the body and will not be available for building muscle. Hence it is important to balance the foods.

This food balance is especially important at breakfast-time. An empty stomach makes a child tired, listless and unable to concentrate. Children who come to school with no breakfast seem by no means rare. It has been shown recently that 20 per cent of children from northern towns and cities come with no breakfast. Some of these probably buy sweets and crisps on the way. Poor breakfasts of high carbohydrate alone cause tiredness by mid-morning because the level of sugar in the blood rises fast but falls off again between 10 and 11 a.m. and a craving for more carbohydrate (sweets) returns. A mixed breakfast with high protein content such as egg and toast and marmalade, though expensive, sustains energy for much longer. The blood sugar level rises only slowly and stays up for three to four hours until dinner-time.

Vitamins and mineral salts
In this book I shall only be dealing with iron. Lack of iron in the diet makes for weakness and lack of resistance to disease due to anaemia. Iron is present in plenty in red meat and in spinach and whole grain. Unfortunately, the iron in vegetable and grain is in a form that is not easily absorbed by the body, so these are not good sources. The iron in red meat is readily available.

One vital need in a baby is for iron. At birth a baby usually has an iron store which will last three or four months – if the mother has been well nourished. So it is important to supplement human (and cow's) milk with food rich in iron: minced liver, broths and gravy.

Social class and height
This chapter began by relating the height of children to the kind of life they lead. It is not just a mechanical matter of good food and

money. The number of children in the family, whether father is in regular work, whether the home is a happy one, whether the mother has looked after herself and the baby before it was born and afterwards – all these factors touch on growth. Comparisons of average heights of children between different segments of a population – the 'social classes' – tell us much about social conditions. Thus in 1874, ten-year-old sons of manual workers in Britain were on average seven centimetres shorter than the ten-year-old sons of gentlemen. But incredibly, a century later, although all ten-year-old boys have become taller and the gap in average height between poor and rich has narrowed, it has not disappeared. In one study of all *short* children at ten in a nothern city, most came from social classes IV and V and had been brought up in poor conditions. In another group of town children at fifteen, children in social classes I and II were taller on average by 4·5 centimetres and 4·4 kilograms heavier than children in the two lowest social classes.

Apart from Sweden, the height (and weight) gap persists in every industrialized country in the world, pointing to the persistence of what Professor Tanner calls the 'stubborn apartheid of an inflexible social structure'.

To sum up: the best practical advice for healthy normal growth in a child is good balance, not only in diet but also in the home. A child needs fairness and encouragement and congratulation when success is achieved, however small. Pleasure and interest in what the child is doing are key factors too in security and in healthy growth. Don't set goals for a child that he can never reach. Don't make him anxious by letting him hear adult quarrels and threats. Persistent unhappiness and insecurity in this country, where food is not short, are considerable factors in preventing proper growth. Time and patience are just as important as food.

Reference

TANNER, J. M. (1961) *Education and Physical Growth* University of London Press

TANNER J. M. (1976) The Long and the Short of it *The Observer* December 19th

Chapter 3

Keeping children healthy

In 1866 Florence Nightingale was asked to open a new children's hospital in Manchester. In her brief and blunt way she wrote and turned down the invitation. She thought that 'building more children's hospitals is not the proper remedy for infantile mortality and sickness – the true remedy for infantile mortality lies in improving the children's homes.' She was right in her priorities. To build a hospital among slums with their overcrowding, malnutrition and insanitary conditions was to put the cart before the horse.

Health and social advance

Most of the progress we enjoy in health now is due to social (and a little to educational) advance. Only recently has medicine played a part. Social advance includes the provision of safe, clean drinking-water and good wholesome food. In the 1850s for example, bread was a crutch to the grave rather than a staff of life for it was often whitened with alum so that the baker was able to pass off a loaf made with cheap flour as a top quality one and make more money. Other improvements have been the removal of human excreta by proper sewage arrangements from rooms, streets and alleyways crowded with people; the change from woollen to boilable cotton clothes so that germs, bugs and lice could be killed; and the demolition of slums. In 1870 came an Act which introduced compulsory education for all children, and at the turn of the century the school health service was born and maternal and child welfare services were introduced to help and advise mothers and protect children's health. All this was an improvement in knowledge and simple cleanliness.

Social advance of various kinds went on right up to 1939, the start of the second world war. Since the start of the war, big and important improvements have come about in child health because of immunisation against diphtheria, whooping cough, measles etc., and the development of antibiotics to combat bacterial diseases like pneumonia. They have made the old terrors – the 'infectious fevers' of the past – pale into insignificance. The poorer countries of the world have health problems rather like ours of a century ago: whooping cough, diphtheria, polio, measles, tetanus and TB disable twelve million children each year; and five million die of one illness or another. Only 10 per cent of the eighty million children born each year in these countries were immunised against the six diseases.

This is *not* to say that everything is roses in Great Britain. There are still acute and serious illnesses which kill many children each year – pneumonia, bronchitis, cancer, gastroenteritis, to name but four – and of course accidents top the list of the causes of death in children aged one to fourteen. The children in the lowest social classes suffer more commonly from such illnesses as pneumonia and bronchitis. These children who grow up in poverty and squalor, who are neglected or handicapped in some way, face greater odds than other children against suffering from physical and mental illness.

This chapter is concerned with the *prevention* of disease and accidents in childhood: unsafe homes and dangerous roads can kill and injure, and family break-ups or neglect and abuse by parents can tell on health and growth as we have seen. Overeating, smoking, drinking and sloth can lead to major disease in later life. Childhood may be a vital time to start prevention of such killers as heart attack, stroke and lung cancer.

Our health is largely in our own hands

To a large extent the prevention of major killers like lung cancer, stroke and heart attack are in our own hands. The incidence of these diseases is now so serious that if a black dot was made for each 1,000 deaths caused by the three captains of death, and the dots plotted over Europe and North America, both continents would be covered in a cloak of darkness just as bad as the plagues of old.

Heart disease

Death from heart attack (coronary heart disease or CHD) has increased in frequency as a cause of death and illness in middle age over the past twenty-five years. The worry is that it is spreading to younger and younger age groups and men in their thirties have begun to be struck down.

The causes of CHD are multiple. Heredity is important but that is beyond our control; we cannot choose our parents. There are, however, risk factors which we *can* do something about. These include high amounts of fats in the blood, cigarette smoking which increases heart rate and blood pressure; fatness; high blood pressure itself and sloth. All of these conditions occur in children and since disease of the arteries can start in early childhood, altering our lifestyle a little early on may help to delay the development of furred-up arteries. A healthy artery has a smooth inner lining which prevents the formation of blood clots that may lead to heart attack or stroke.

It may seem surprising but fatty streaks have been found in the heart's arteries in babies of three to four months. They become relatively common at five years. Possibly the fatty streaks can be reabsorbed and vanish at this age but later in life the raised patches which arise on the artery walls of some people may have their origin in the fatty streaks. These can lead to the dangerous blood clots.

What practical things can we do to lower the risk? Many children are overweight in industrial countries like our own. About one quarter of babies in England are likely to be bonny and bouncing, i.e. too fat, in their first year of life. In early school years there are not all that many fat children. The figure for primary-age children is about six in a hundred. At adolescence, however, the percentage increases, especially among girls.

Though we cannot be too precise, a good many fat children turn into fat adults. One study in Birmingham showed that eight out of ten fat children continued to be plump when they grew up. These fat children are more likely to have higher blood pressure than children of normal weight because they are carrying a bigger load. In some cases they may have higher levels of fatty substances in the blood especially at adolescence which may lead to the furring-up of the arteries. Fat children move more slowly and sit about more. The dice are certainly loaded against them.

There are hereditary tendencies to fatness in some families but more obesity is self-made or parent-made. Helen Bruch, an eminent American psychologist, wrote (in Greene 1971): 'show me a fat child and I will show you a disturbed home.' Often a fat child has been coddled too much: sweets as rewards; no sweets for punishment. Unhappiness from any cause, school or home life, may lead a child to comfort in eating, just as a man will go off to the pub for a pint. From what I have said it is clear that the causes of fatness are not well understood. But the only way to lose weight is to eat less.

Most fat babies are bottle fed. It is easy to think that a baby is still hungry after his bottle when really he may be thirsty or have wind. Breast feeding produces fewer fat babies and has other advantages already discussed. The main disadvantage of obesity in infancy is a tendency to chest infections. The fact that fat babies are an increasing problem is reflected in the larger scales that have become necessary at many clinics over the past few years!

Fat in the diet

Improved standards of living have brought a higher consumption of milk, butter, cream, cheese and meat and consequently, of fat. This has the effect of boosting the level of cholesterol in the blood and cholesterol is under suspicion as a blood-fat linked with CHD. In fact the risk of developing CHD increases steadily with increasing levels of cholesterol.

Fat intake need not be cut to extremes but it is worth noting in Table 3 (below) the fat content of the war-time rations for one person for a week in 1944.

Table 3 A week's war-time rations for one person

Bacon and ham	4 oz
Sugar	8 oz
Tea	2 oz
Meat	1s 2d worth
Cheese	2 oz
Butter	2 oz
Margarine	4 oz
Cooking fat	2 oz
Shell eggs	1 egg per 2 wks
Dried eggs	1 pkt per 4 wks
Liquid milk	2½ pt
Sweets	12 oz per 4 wks

The ration was small compared with consumption now but the population was healthy. Much expert opinion suggests that no more than one-third of calories for growing children should come from fatty foods like butter, cheese and fatty meat. Remember that a boy of ten needs about 2,500 Kcals a day and a girl slightly less; 28·35 grams (one ounce) of butter contains 226 Kcals, cheese 120, bacon 115, pork 119. It does not take much butter and cheese to give 800 Kcals and most of us eat too much. It is wise to cut down the intake of these foods and fatty meat. Grilling is healthier than frying for many foods. Fruit, carbohydrate-rich foods like bread and potatoes, can be substituted for and balanced with fat calories. Eggs contain a lot of cholesterol (about 250 milligrams each) but one egg daily is unlikely to be harmful.

Exercise

One risk factor in developing CHD (perhaps the only one that doctors agree about) is lack of exercise. Regular exercise helps to maintain a healthy weight and to keep blood pressure and cholesterol levels down. Children today, as well as their parents, do not walk much or take good regular exercise in other forms. A study of teenage girls in the States showed that less than one hour a day was spent in moderate activity. The rest of their time when not asleep was spent sitting, either travelling to school, at school, or at home watching TV.

Think back to grandfather's days. He probably did not have heart trouble, at least until his sixties. It is likely that the heavy physical work done by many people in those days not only developed brawny arm muscles but also strengthened their heart muscles and kept their arteries open. Even quite well-off people walked to work. They had stout boots and shoes in place of the flimsy fashion shoes of today. Their health problems were, of course, different and related to poverty, slums, grinding work and poor food. The rural people were often worse off than folk in towns and the farm labourer the worst fed of all:

> He used to tramp off to work while town folk were abed
> With nothing in his belly but a slice or two of bread;
> He dined upon potatoes, and he never dreamed of meat
> Except a lump of bacon fat sometimes by way of treat

For children today exercise habits need to be established that continue after school and beyond; walking and cycling and small group activities like golf or tennis. The team games and physical education of school are unlikely to continue and must be replaced. There is a tendency among those who stood miserably inactive in the rain during team games to opt out of exercise altogether in late adolescence. This is when bad habits are formed; it could be a time to start new, good habits.

Smoking

Lung cancer, too, is a modern epidemic. Cigarette smoking is without doubt a direct cause of the disease, but air pollution by coal smoke, exhaust fumes and other industrial pollution may play their part. Smoking by very young children is not a major worry to parents, but many children start smoking even before ten and the habit increases greatly in adolescence. In fact one in three smokers start before the age of nine, some even as young as five. About 34 per cent of boys aged fifteen smoke and two-thirds this number of girls. By this time the habit has got a hold, partly because nicotine is one of the most dependence-producing drugs known. Many factors start the smoking habit in children: availability of cigarettes; curiosity; rebelliousness; wanting to appear tough; anticipation of adulthood; the example of parents and teachers, friends, brothers and sisters.

The evidence is piled high that smoking causes or worsens lung cancer, chronic bronchitis and CHD: tar, nicotine and carbon monoxide, all contained and produced by cigarettes, are the culprits. The recent Royal College of Physicians report *Smoking or Health?* (1977) contains important sections on the smoking habits of children and the possible effects on their future health. These include a twenty-fold increase in the risk of lung cancer in heavy smokers and an increase of about three and a half times in the risk of dying from CHD. The Royal College's report states that 'on average the time by which an habitual smoker's life is shortened is about five and a half minutes for each cigarette smoked.' Some smokers will do better than this, some worse. Some smokers will live to a ripe old age but some will die young. As a group, smokers of twenty cigarettes a day will live about five years less than a similar group of nonsmokers.

We have seen in Chapter 1 that smoking is also a hazard to the health and well-being of the unborn baby. Recent evidence from Sweden based on highly magnified pictures of cells in the umbilical artery, which carries food to and oxygen from mother to baby, show a big difference between smokers and nonsmokers. In the non-smoking mothers, cells in the umbilical artery seem to be arranged in an orderly manner. In women who smoke between ten and sixty cigarettes a day, there is a cobblestone effect: the surfaces of the cells look worn and bubbly like old cobbles. Within the fine structure of these cells, ultramicroscope pictures show changes. Similar changes have also been noted in the blood vessels of the placenta. If these changes are mirrored by changes in the foetal blood vessels, there could be long-term risk to the baby. Damage to artery walls might aid the build-up of fatty deposits in the blood vessels mentioned on page 38. In other words, the prevention of CHD might start *before* birth.

Bad teeth

Dental decay is at disease level in this country. The scale of the problem is vast. A recent Government dental health survey on children aged between five and fifteen reckoned that six million out of nine million school children are in need of treatment. Of children aged five, only 30 per cent had sound teeth and another 30 per cent had five or more bad teeth. By eight only 15 per cent had a good set of teeth, while at fourteen, only 4 per cent had good teeth and seven out of ten children had five or more bad teeth. By sixteen one-third of children had lost one or more permanent teeth. The cause is a combination of sweet, sticky foods, and the poor dental hygiene which often has a low priority in the scale of family discipline. Before the age of five children's teeth can be rotted by the continued use of a dummy filled with fruit syrup as a comforter. The persistent use after weaning of a bottle containing sweetened milk or orange juice can have the same effect. It seems ridiculous to have to point this out.

If children plead for biscuit money at break, offer an orange, apple, or banana instead. Brushing teeth under supervision two or three times a day is important for young children's teeth. By the time they are eight there is no need to supervise.

One practical cheap and safe measure that could be taken to sub-stantially reduce tooth decay in children and slow it in adults would be the addition of tiny traces of fluoride to all public water supplies. But even if we do not add it to water, you can buy fluoride tablets from the chemist and these will help to give stronger teeth to children if taken up to the age of twelve or fourteen.

Accidents

It was Stina Sandels (1968) in *Children in Traffic* who asked her seven-year-old niece how she managed to cross the road on the way to school without an adult. The reply from an intelligent, well-trained child was: 'Well, you see, first I look to the right and then to the left and then to the right again. Then I stand there shaking – and then I run.'

If you ask a child of nursery and primary age *what* they are frightened of and *why*, half of the three- to seven-year-olds, and a third of the ten-year-olds, will say they are most scared on their way to and from school and 'because of the traffic'. To judge speed of cars and the complexity of the traffic environment is very difficult for a small child. And of course when small children become aroused by the sight of a friend across the road, or by a thought, they become so taken up with their feelings that everything else ceases to exist for them.

Table 4 (below) shows that death from road accidents forms the single largest group and home accidents a substantial group, especially of very young children. Deaths from falls from windows or buildings and from fire form a smaller but still worrying group. Poisoning is a rare cause of death but the small figure in the table does not reflect the concern and anxiety caused by accidental poisoning which results in about 160,000 hospital admissions a year. The use of child-resistant containers should cut down this number as their use becomes more widespread.

Table 4 Some causes of accidental death in childhood (England and Wales, 1973)

	Age (years)			Total
	0–4	5–9	10–14	
Total accidental deaths	881	516	380	1,777
All road accidents	193	332	201	726
(Involving pedestrians)	132	258	118	508
(Involving cyclists)	6	22	38	66

43

Table 4 continued

	Age (years)			Total
	0–4	5–9	10–14	
All home accidents	363	41	33	437
All falls	56	24	21	101
(Falls from buildings)	19	6	6	31
All burns	103	27	13	143
(Conflagration)	73	24	9	106
Drowning	78	73	47	198
Inhalation and ingestion	183	6	3	192
Homicide and injury purposefully inflicted	74	14	14	102
Suffocation	60	7	17	84
Poisoning	29	1	4	34
Electrocution	12	2	4	18

(From R. H. Jackson (Ed) (1977) *Children, the Environment and Accidents* Pitman Medical.)

Table 5 Home accidents recorded by Accident and Emergency Departments. Distribution by location of accident (Figures are expressed as percentages)

Location	Age	
	0–4	5–14
Kitchen	19·8	16·6
Living and dining-room	36·0	23·3
Outside	14·2	27·5
Stairs	9·6	11·1
Bedroom	10·9	9·9
Bathroom and toilet	3·4	3·6
Hall	3·4	4·8
Garage	0·6	1·0
Other	2·1	2·2
Total	100·0	100·0

(From R. H. Jackson (Ed) (1977) *Children, the Environment and Accidents* Pitman Medical.)

Table 6 Home accidents recorded by Accident and Emergency Departments. Product groups associated with accidents in the 0–4 age group

	Number of cases reported
Household furniture	412
Construction	213
Kitchen utensils	129
Cleaning products	89
Plants and trees	81
Playthings and sports equipment	80
DIY/Household maintenance	76
Outside environment	71
Flammable and corrosive liquids	70
Household fixtures	68

(From R. H. Jackson (Ed) (1977) *Children, the Environment and Accidents* Pitman Medical.)

Tables 5 and 6 (above) record the location of accidents. For the under-fives the largest number happens surprisingly in the living or dining room, about one-fifth in the kitchen and large numbers in the bedroom and outside. With the preschool child (Table 6) falls from furniture – chairs, beds, tables – top the list. Second come accidents on stairs, trapping fingers in a door or falling from a window. Third are accidents with kitchen equipment – teapots and kettles, wringers and spindryers.

The list is endless. As far as traffic is concerned, no child in the vulnerable age group of four to eight should be out in the street alone. Those who want sound advice on this point should read *Children in Traffic*. But the basic aim is to give children a sound traffic training which can be steadily developed simply because children will spend much time in heavy traffic and most will ride bicycles. Here are a few simple rules:

1   Make sure that a child does not have to rush to school because he is late.
2   Teach children the habit of crossing on zebra crossings.

3 Teach them to understand and respect traffic signals.
4 Set a good example in traffic because children copy actions rather than listen to explanations.
5 See to it that their bikes are in good order.
6 Never let them out on their bikes alone before the age of nine.

But in the last analysis it is adults who are to blame for child accidents. Drivers need to be taught about the behaviour of children in traffic. Other hazards are bad planning of busy roads near schools, shortage of playgrounds protected from traffic, and pedestrian ways separated from car traffic.

As far as domestic accidents are concerned, a young child under five should never be far from an adult. Nor is it natural for him to be alone. Instinctively, that is biologically, a child wants to be near 'special companions', usually mother; this is an inborn feeling forged in an environment which, though different from and fiercer than our own, was nevertheless protective.

This chapter has probably only told you what you know in your bones already; that sound habits of health start early and childhood is an optimum time to begin good behavioural patterns to prevent later disease. The only intelligent medicine is preventive. So here are some rules for health for you and your children.

1 The most important single factor which parents need to ponder is cigarette smoking. If they smoke it not only hurts an unborn child but other children are likely to smoke. Smoking is dangerous. Also if you smoke you may not handle a baby enough for fear of dropping ash on his face and clothes.
2 Take exercise. If you like walking or cycling and don't overkill it by making it a bore, your children are more likely to enjoy taking exercise.
3 Keep on the thin side. You should never be shocked to see a child's ribs showing, it is healthier that way.
4 Watch the diet and don't eat or give the family too much fat.
5 Cut out sweet, sugary foods; they are bad for the teeth and contain masses of 'empty' calories.
6 Do not encourage children to develop strong likes and dislikes

about food. It is better to expect children to eat what is provided without commenting on what they 'like'.

7 Encourage handwashing before eating – good old-fashioned simple cleanliness.

8 Even though you become a bore, warn of the dangers of the road. Keep an eye on young children playing; the home can be hazardous to infants and toddlers so take sensible precautions.

References

GREENE, R. (1971) *Human Hormones* World University Library
ROYAL COLLEGE OF PHYSICIANS (1977) *Smoking or Health?* Pitman Medical Books
SANDELS, S. (1968) *Children in Traffic* Elek

Chapter 4

Talking

Like the body the brain needs food and exercise of a kind. Over-crowding, lack of play materials, lack of stimulus and lack of conversation, are all indicators of persistent underprivilege and can hurt the mind just as smoking can damage the heart and lungs. It is easy to be concerned only with the physical health of children but mental and intellectual health are as important. Indeed, physical, emotional and mental health are all bound up with each other.

Speech – a basic human need

Speech, like good food and fresh air, is a basic human need. If a child is starved of speech at a critical time of life he may be damaged. He may even be dumb for life if not spoken to by the age of seven or eight (some say by twelve or thirteen). It thus seems that there is an optimum time for the developing brain to master the skill of talking.

The story of the Wild Boy of Aveyron throws light on critical times for language development. The Wild Boy was captured in the forest when he was about eleven or twelve years old, in 1799. He was a child without language but was at first thought to be deaf, since he showed very little reaction to quite loud sounds. Then it was realized that in fact his hearing was acute, but that he only paid attention to sounds which meant something to him, like the noise of cracking walnuts, a food which he liked. His sense of smell was sharp but his vision could not at first distinguish between objects that were painted and objects in relief.

As I have suggested, we do not know for certain whether man has critical times in his development for the acquisition of oral language, but experience in teaching the Wild Boy and others like him suggest that if a child hasn't learned verbal communication at an early age he never will, or will at best be very backward. Moreover, children who have learned to speak may actually lose the facility if they are isolated for long periods.

The Wild Boy may have suffered from a form of sensory deprivation consequent upon his isolation. He only paid attention, both tactually and auditorily, to what immediately concerned him – food. So far as one can tell, he was not unintelligent; but his discriminatory faculties, like his speech, had not developed because nothing in the environment had stimulated them. The brain needs to learn by experience in a two-way dynamic relationship with the environment as this story shows.

The remarkable story of Genie re-emphasizes what was said earlier about the marvellous resilience of the human brain. From the age of twenty months until her admission to hospital at 13 years 9 months in 1972, Genie suffered terrible deprivation – isolated in a small, closed room, tied to a potty chair where she remained nearly all the time, sometimes all night. If she made a sound she was beaten. Her father and brother never spoke to her but barked at her like dogs. Her mother was forbidden to speak and was allowed to spend no more than a few minutes with her during feeding. Genie was a prisoner with no language for the eleven crucial years between two and puberty. But she can now speak simply through exposure to talk. She is, of course, very backward – at sixteen she talks like a two- to three-year-old, but understands much more. Her progress is slow and it is uncertain how far it will progress. It seems as if Genie had a normal brain at birth, was right-handed and that her left hemisphere was ready to develop language (see page 52). But because she received no language stimulus the left hemisphere's development was inhibited. What meagre stimulus she obtained was through her eyes. One imagines her sitting day after day, week after week, year after year, taking in every visual stimulus, every crack in the paint, every slight change of colour and form. This visual stimulus was sufficient for her right hemisphere to develop normally since it rather than the left is more involved with understanding the environment. From the results of complex tests it seems as if Genie's right hemisphere is doing all the work in language and the left hemisphere (the analytical side involved in language and number) remains underdeveloped. I shall say more about the left and right hemispheres in Chapter 7.

All this confirms that the brain learns by experience. Give plenty to your child. It also underlines the brain's astonishing capabilities and adaptability. Perhaps, though, if Genie had been born a boy, her brain would not have had quite such plasticity and she might have never talked (see page 92).

There are a few interesting stories from history about the search for the origins of language.

In the fifth century BC the Greek historian Herodotus reported that the Egyptian Pharaoh Psammetichus (664–610 BC) sought to determine the most primitive 'natural language' by placing two infants in an isolated mountain hut to be cared for by a servant who was cautioned not to speak in their presence on pain of death. According to the story, the first word uttered was 'bekos', the Phrygian word for 'bread', which convinced the Pharaoh that this was the original language. James IV of Scotland (1473–1513) is reported to have attempted the same 'experiment'. The Scottish children, however, were said to 'spak very guid Ebrew'. Two hundred years before James, the Holy Roman Emperor Frederick II of Hohenstaufen was said to have carried out a similar test but the children died before they spoke at all.

Clearly in these tales more than speech was missing, because deaf children can develop happily. What seemed to be absent was good *mothering* which gives all the love and comfort besides talking. Children in foundling homes when compared with children in a prison nursery who could see and play with their mothers, were found to have deteriorated intellectually; the intellect started to worsen when one nurse had to look after eight children. Some wise doctor in the past commented simply that taking away a child from his mother or another he loves, breaks his heart.

The brain is cued to learn language

We now know what Herodotus and James IV did not; that babies are not born readymade to speak Greek, Hebrew or Scottish. In theory they could make all the noises in all the languages of the world and they could learn any language if they started early enough. If a baby is listened to carefully he babbles with the sounds he hears his parents making. By six months a baby will have picked up the speech rhythms of his parents and their intonation. If he has not he must be very deaf. In fact, deafness can be diagnosed before the age of one by testing a baby's speech rhythms.

This ability to pick up sounds and rhythms early shows the sensitivity of the young brain and nervous system. In the five years from birth during the time when the brain is growing fast, a child is absorbing language fast so that by five he is fluent. He loves reciting and singing rhymes and jingles, besides enjoying stories and acting them out in detail alone or with friends. He can usually give his full name, age and address and often his birthday. In five short years this really stunning intellectual achievement is routinely performed by every preschool child. How sharply he must listen and watch! Even at four a child can change his style of speech depending on whether he is talking to his mother or pretending to be the doctor. Even at two notice how he will subtly change his style of speech to talk to the baby.

At five, not only is his brain highly advanced, in fact 90 per cent grown, but his speech organs are well developed. Incredibly his jaw length is much the same as that of an adult. His brain and speech apparatus, his senses and his exploring hands are all geared to learn.

It is important for parents to know this and to have high expectations of a child. Give him plenty of time and patience. Young children are rather like mirrors and reflect what goes on around them, not only speech patterns but quality of speech, attitudes and values. They need a good and continuing model.

The brain is poised to learn speech
What special features of the brain make a child a specialist in learning to speak?

First, a simple observation of the brain of a new-born baby shows that the left half of the cortex where language is developed is bigger than the right half. The speech 'bump' persists in adults and suggests that a baby is born with a brain poised to learn speech and all it needs is words to set everything in motion.

Second, the parts of the human brain which help to give delicate control to the tongue, jaws and lips are big in proportion to the parts that control movement in other parts of the body. In fact, a quarter of the motor cortex of the human brain is set aside for speech and control of speech muscles. So the importance of speech to man is reflected in the amount of the motor area made over to it.

Third, large areas of the grey matter which is the human thinking cap are uncommitted and need to be filled with experience including language. Within a few months from birth a baby recognizes concepts – a dog, a cat, a bird, a flower. He hears his mother speaking words that describe the concept – 'dog', and soon he is writing on the blank slate of his mind, or in other words 'programming' a large area of the uncommitted cortex for speech. If he is going to be right-handed he is most likely setting up the speech mechanism in the left hemisphere. The idea of a 'blank slate' should not mislead. The brain is living and develops its powers by practice – a notion far removed from a 'passive' slate.

Fourth, the nerve pathways in the brain between the areas for hearing, touching, smelling and the areas for memory are profuse. These crossconnecting nerve pathways are so numerous that a special switching mechanism like a telephone exchange has developed just behind the temple which helps to make connections between vital parts of the brain cortex. Injury to this essential part of the brain can produce curious jumbling up of speech because of difficulties in making the right links between things heard and things seen.

These profuse nerve links in a child's brain help him to connect the *concept* of something with the *sound* of the word. Thus he sees a black, oddly-shaped thing with a waving tail – the cat concept – and connects this with the sound of the word 'pussy' his mother makes. When the nerve pathways between the 'concept unit' and the 'sound unit' have been made the child *understands*. Understanding shines in his eyes long before he can speak. The programming of the sound unit goes on in the left hemisphere if the child is right-handed. The nonverbal 'concept' – pussy – is programmed in the temporal (memory) lobes of the grey matter (see Chapter 6 and Figure 5, page 76) and is used to match a memory of something (in this case a cat) with a new experience of a cat.

A child understands before he can speak because the brain machinery has not developed far enough for words to be uttered. At about eighteen months to two years he can make the sound 'pussy' and link words into speech because by then the motor cortex has developed far enough to bring into play the speech apparatus used to pronounce the word. It is as if the brain is building up to a springboard of nerve development from which speech can take off.

When a real cat appears, how and why does a child say the word 'cat' aloud and perhaps laugh in triumph at the pleasure of saying it?

The first time he hears the word and the brain machinery is advanced enough for him to utter, he imitates it. Then perhaps a cat really appears on silent paws, tail pluming. The brain mechanism carries a patterned nerve message of this cat to the memory system in the temporal lobes of the cortex which act like Aladdin's lamp out of which a memory about a cat appears. The mind compares the two images – this cat now and what is remembered about cats – and sees a similarity. Then another patterned nerve message is formed, made up of the remembered concept of a cat modified by the fresh experience of one, and is flashed to the speech mechanism and the 'word unit' lights up in the mind. Then the child acts. A signal is flashed to the speech area of the motor cortex which commands the speech organs to work. He says 'cat' out aloud.

As everyone knows who has been woken in the morning by 'da-da-da-da-da', a baby practises the sounds he hears. He experiments with them, even plays with them, and thus refines and sharpens the 'word units' in his brain. He is helped by approval and an appreciative audience. So although it is sometimes maddening, do encourage him.

It should be clear by now that there is a lot we do not know about speech. When a child sees a butterfly his brain has to interpret the picture of this fluttering, coloured thing. But how the right concept is picked out from the thousands stored away in the concept mechanism, presented for the mind to 'approve', and then, in a flash, telegraphed to the speech areas of the cortex for the child to utter the word describing the concept, is a mystery. Nor do we know how a child analyses 'regularities' in the language, sees order, and uses old words again in new combinations he has never heard before.

The gift of speech can rust
There is one necessary condition for a child's poised brain to learn speech – he must have continuous and lengthy lessons from an expert, usually his mother. If she does not bother then speech, like growth, will tend to be backward. In language deprivation we should perhaps remember especially the rural child brought up on an isolated farm or hamlet. I reckon that rural deprivation is often worse

than urban with some children coming to school at five with only 400 or 500 words instead of over 2,000. But to keep this in perspective, only about five in every hundred five-year-olds speak so poorly that they are unable to make themselves understood by strangers, and only one in every hundred is using incomplete sentences. These figures include retarded children and those with hearing loss.

How do parents, and especially the mother, teach language? The same direct method is used everywhere – the mother talks to the child before he can understand. Before he speaks she is on the lookout for understanding. When he says his first words he is encouraged by an admiring audience. And the first understanding of the mother tongue is made easier by the habit mothers have of repeating the same phrases with slight alterations and, at the same time, doing the thing they are talking about: 'When I get up in the morning this is what I'll do, I'll wash my face, brush my teeth. . . .' Language for the child is direct. He uses it to get what he wants, to understand facts about toys, animals, books. He uses language, not as an end in itself, but to learn about life and to share his ideas with others. So talk to a baby and talk in phrases – instead of 'pussy, pussy', say 'Look there's a pussy cat'; or to a four-year-old, 'What would pussy do if a dog came?' Make what you are doing together productive: lead on, encourage. It is the same when the child is older. 'Shut-up' answers instead of dialogue about books, toys, animals, can rust the development of language.

Since a child's mother is usually the 'expert' who teaches him to talk, it is obvious that language development depends greatly on the quality of mothering, starting at birth. Good mothering in turn depends on a subtle interaction between the mother (or mother-figure) and child, where the mother recognizes the cues and signals in the child's babbling, clinging, grasping, crying, smiling, and responds to them in appropriate ways. Insensitivity of a mother to a child's signals dulls that interaction and keeps it on a concrete level simply because the child gets discouraged and only sends out the obvious signals. Sensitivity to the child's nonverbal cues stimulates increasing levels of communication between them, giving the richest opportunities for the growth and development of language, and indeed other capacities.

A successful mother and father will *believe* that a child of less than a year old is capable of taking initiative and sharing joint enterprises. A dull or retarded mother, or simply and more commonly, a distracted, tired mother, is not sufficiently sensitive to a child's signals and failure to observe these keeps the child's development on a dull level. She will tend to think of children as passive and without initiative. Much of importance in the development of the intellect depends on good mothering and high levels of expectation. For instance, when a baby is having its milk, it gulps and gurgles, and pauses. The mother smiles and says, 'Yes, it's lovely isn't it, would you like more?' The baby has simply paused and the mother's sentence is complicated. But the baby goes back to the milk eagerly and laughs and the mother *believes* that he has understood her. Only by these tiny assumptions about understanding and intelligence does the baby begin to acquire these qualities.

The expectation level of mothers and those looking after young children is crucial to language development and general intelligence. If the language environment of a child is against him, he can learn not to ask questions. He thinks that adults are there for giving orders, he does not seek explanations. Readiness for reading is lacking; guessing what comes next in the story, and the experience of interpreting pictures are missing, to the great disadvantage of the child and its brain development.

The level of expectation needs to be high particularly for so-called 'deprived' children who perhaps have had too much warm, even smothering affection, to compensate for their background. Their experience may have been rich and varied in its own way and should be used to develop their intellectual strengths. One difference between 'advantaged' and 'disadvantaged' children is that 'advantaged' parents read more to their children and give more explanations.

For language to be enriched, experience must be provided, often in specially-created situations. Young children do not learn only by the light of nature; intervention by adults at the right time is very necessary. This need not be complicated. In *Lark Rise to Candleford*, Flora Thompson remarks: 'The hedgerow' (or garden) 'is so crammed with interest that it would provide studies for more hours than there are in the day'; looking into the mouth of a foxglove at the honey guides and stamens, and a bee with fat honey bags cramming itself down to get the nectar; watching ants scurrying over your shoes and trying to entice one onto a blade of grass, then onto a flower; watching one carry its stick load, like a miniature digger; following the mysterious rustlings in the hedgerow; or watching an alert spider on a new-spun web; or a rainbow forming and dissolving. Lenses, magnets and clockwork toys, too, are fascinating experiences for a child which involve talk, observation and even drawing conclusions – analysis as well as fantasy and imagination. And the mundane, everyday things like washing hands can help a child to use his senses if an adult helps him think about what he is doing: 'What colour is the soap? Is it soft or hard? Listen to your soapy hands.'

In Victorian times (and in the 1930s in my boyhood) lots of family word, alphabet, memory and improvised story games were played as well as counting games, card games and spelling bees. Perhaps in the rush we have forgotten them or no longer have time to play them and turn on the TV as a soft option or, despising memory work, have thrown the baby out with the bathwater. But a hundred years ago, judging from books of children's games published by quite modest publishers, ordinary families seemed dauntingly articulate. Perhaps we should look them up or ask Grandma about them. (Two good source books are listed at the end of the chapter.) Perhaps you will remember these games vaguely. Use them.

Sign language
I mentioned earlier in this chapter the need for a mother to recognize the 'signals' in a child's behaviour, how he stands, the way he uses his hands, his eye movements and facial expressions – for a child's looks and behaviour speak words. I also stressed that interaction between mother and child is crucial to sound development; the mother must recognize the baby's signals and react to them.

The young of our species have a relatively poor instinctive behaviour repertoire (though richer than has often been assumed) so the matrix of movements, signals, sensitivity to signals and motivations is improved by interaction and learning more than in any other animal species. Of course, the way a mother interacts with a child is not 'studied'. Stroking a child's head as he stands beside her is a brief signal of recognition and affection in a situation where smiles are unlikely but this is done 'without thinking'. It maintains contact where in other situations a smile would suffice.

It was Charles Darwin (1872) a century ago who first studied behaviour scientifically and set down his observations in his book *The Expression of the Emotions in Man and Animals*. This is what he wrote about language and 'nonverbal' language:

> The power of communication between members of the same tribe by means of language has been of paramount importance in the development of man; and the force of language is much aided by the expressive movements of the face and body. We perceive this at once when we converse on any important subject with any person whose face is concealed.

A third party watching the greetings of two people from a distance but unable to hear the conversation would be able to tell a good deal about the personalities and their relationship. Ethologists (students of animal behaviour) have begun to believe that at least some of the methods (objective descriptions of what animals do and what circumstances bring about their movements) developed in their science could, if both their strengths and weaknesses are borne in mind, profitably be applied to important human problems such as the social interaction of children, at first with the mother, then with peers, and then with an even wider circle.

Results from this kind of analysis are comforting because they confirm much that we know in our bones already; they may even make us more sensitive and responsive but not, of course, studied in our actions.

The strengthening and maintenance of an infant's repertoire of behaviour demands *feedback* from the environment: a voice, a smile, feeding, rocking, providing warmth and physical comfort. But the baby is no passive partner. He plays a very active role in the development of a close, loving attachment with his mother. This, rather than stimulation by the mother or the passive satisfaction of creature-comfort needs, is the real base of attachment. Early on a baby cries when held by someone other than his mother. It is his signal of distress when insecure or in pain. When he is returned to his mother his signal has worked: it has had the effect of reducing the distance between them. And a baby smiles more readily and more often and gurgles and burbles more when held by her alone. As the direct cuddling and caretaking of the mother weakens, a type of behaviour develops which puts the mother 'in the mood to be with her baby' – eye contact. It is to this potent signal that the baby of four weeks directs his gaze. And he reads her face like a map. Children of three to four months react fearfully to a sober-faced mother which all suggests that smiling with mouth and eyes has a reassuring effect on an infant. At five months a baby greets his mother after an absence by lifting his arms, smiling and crowing with delight. And later, at nearly a year, by clapping his hands in greeting while smiling and gurgling. All these and many other 'bonding' behaviours demand feedback from the parents. A cold response, or a wooden one, with little physical contact, or one that underestimates the potentialities of the child will not stimulate him or give him the security to become 'attached' to others who play with him – father, brothers and sisters. A mother, for instance, who hugs a child then boisterously throws him in the air after he has approached with oblique eyebrows and a droopy mouth instead of lifting him and holding him steadily until he lifts his head to look around, is responding quite inappropriately.

Somebody said a child is not a pot to be filled with information but a fire to be lit. Biologically it is right to arouse and stimulate exploratory interest in the young, and from a very early age. And for this to happen parents have to be sensitive to a child's nonverbal signals. The smile, the grin, the frown, the fixed stare, the panic and the angry face; the 'pain-' and 'hunger-cry' in babies; the squeals, the short and high-pitched sounds during exciting nursery games, all tell a tale as do gestures.

Let us return to speech and a final cautionary word. Don't pound a child with questions. There is a silent pleasure in looking, smelling, feeling and listening, which is destroyed by too much well-meant interference with books and explanations. Children know when they are being 'instructed' and may begin to hate the sight of books.

To summarize: the brain is a marvellous instrument for language learning. A baby is born with his brain poised to learn speech. Don't let the natural gift rust. Talk naturally, ask questions, listen and give him time to answer. Make time to do things together. Time and patience are just about the most valuable things you can give him.

From small beginnings in the home and school, language can

soon pass from the simple, practical role of giving and receiving instructions. This is what Eugene Ionesco wrote about language:

What is the purpose of language? To enable one to express one's thoughts and possibly one's conception of the universe – whence philosophy. To give one a theoretical and practical understanding of necessity – whence science. To enable one to express emotion and feeling – whence art and literature. To give and receive useful instructions we have practical language.

The roots to all these major areas of man's culture are to be found in the experiences that school and home give a child in the early years from birth to puberty.

References

BARNARD, D. ST P. (1977) *The Puffin Book of Car Games* Penguin
IONESCO, E. (1975) Article in *Encounter* October *Mrs Valentine's Games for Family Parties and Children* Warne (1865)
THOMPSON, FLORA (1973) *Lark Rise to Candleford* Penguin

Chapter 5

Learning: the unfolding brain

Man is set apart from other animals by such characteristics as speech, his moral sense, his 'bloody-mindedness', his imagination, his joy and sorrow, and his appreciation of beauty. These qualities which lift him above the beasts manifest themselves in his behaviour which is a function of the brain. We learn about the world through our ears, eyes and sense of touch. And we know that when light falls on the retina, messages of an electrical nature are sent along nerves to the parts of the brain cortex that are known to deal with sight: an accurate copy of the distribution of light on the retina is not passed along nerves but rather a simplified code which somehow the brain turns into a picture. As Russell Brain (1960) wrote many years ago: 'the only necessary condition of the observer's seeing colours, hearing sounds, and experiencing his own body is that the appropriate physiological events shall occur in the appropriate areas of his brain.' This is all rather unsatisfactory and vague but we are as yet in a very primitive stage in our understanding of how the brain works or how it affects behaviour. The outstanding quality of man's brain compared with the brain of other animals seems to be its flexibility and 'openness'.

The open, flexible brain
Heredity sets a limit to what each of us can learn given the best circumstances, but its instructions for most behaviour are only very lightly sketched in. This inherited openness of mind helps us as a species by giving us enormous adjustability and mental resilience to cope with a fast-changing world. By contrast most animals are born and grow up in environments little or no different from that of their parents and grandparents: the rooks in the nearby park have built their nests in the beeches for generations to the same pattern and as

Darwin said in *Origin of Species*, their behaviour is strongly inherited to fit them to their 'conditions of life'.

This inherited flexibility allows each and every one of us to be a bus rather than a tram. But each bus is unique in itself: one has greater acceleration, another better braking power or steering, and so on.

For children most behaviour is learned by trial and error, by imitation, by playing with other children and adults, by playing alone and by the rules parents and teachers set. And the spin-off in behaviour from learning during upbringing can be seen in the values and skills children learn which vary from culture to culture. British children learn to read, write and count, but South American Indian children learn to plant corn, weave cloth and the boys to use toy hunting weapons their fathers give to them. Differences in upbringing lead to differences in behaviour. Children in Northern India learn respect and obedience and are quiet. British and American children learn to be self-sufficient and individualistic. They are more boisterous than Indian children. Evolution has made the brain's capabilities for flexibility in behaviour truly enormous.

Looked at another way, because the young developing mind is flexible, impressionable and open, if children are educationally, socially and culturally deprived, there may be damage to the intellect and emotions caused not necessarily by altering nerve pathways, though this is quite possible, but by creating a poor state of mind which learns to expect nothing much out of life.

A budding scientist
Children begin to explore and experiment and discover very early on as the brain is developing fast. Here is an observation of a one-year-old boy exploring and learning made by the distinguished ethologist Niko Tinbergen (1972):

A twelve-month-old boy, guarded by his aunt and grandmother, was observed crawling about over a sandy slope which was bare but for isolated rosettes of ragwort and occasional thistle plants. After having moved over many ragwort rosettes without showing any reaction to them, he happened to crawl over a thistle, whose prickly leaves slightly scratched his feet. Giving a barely perceptible start, he crawled on at first, but stopped a second or so later, and looked back over his shoulder. Then, moving slightly back, he rubbed his foot once more over the thistle. Next he turned to the plant, looked at it with intense concentration, and moved his hand back and forth over it. This was followed by a perfect control experiment: he looked round, selected a ragwort rosette and touched it in the same way. After this he touched the thistle once more, and only then did he continue his journey. This is only one of many examples of true experimentation in a pre-verbal child of highly sophisticated exploration.

The child was behaving very much like a budding scientist. What all children try to do, is to apply the scientific method to the environment. A child learns the nature of things by such experience. You cannot teach him in words because he does not understand. He experiences the world by touching and looking, he draws his conclusions, then he tests them, just like the child who went back to touch the thistle and the ragwort. This form of building up a stock of knowledge of the world through trial and error is the basis of much later intellectual activity. For *all* children arousing and stimulating interest by creating an environment which invites exploration is sound practice.

For practical purposes it is important to give children maximum sensory experience by making sure they have plenty of things around them to look at and to touch. Texture, for example, is important and fascinating and they soon begin to learn the differences between smooth, rough, and prickly surfaces, as did the baby with the ragwort and the thistle. The human nervous system is adapted marvellously for 'active' touch because man can learn more about the world this way. A shape is far more easily identified correctly when explored and touched by the finger-tips than when pressed into the palm of the hand. A child's exploring fingers are an extension of his eyes.

Brain and environment
It is important *not* to underestimate the natural exploratory drive of a baby and a toddler. It is the way he learns the difference between up and down, space and solid, near and far, smooth and rough, and most other things. To imprison him is like depriving a seed of the

water it needs to sprout and develop. In fact all recent research seems to be underlining the remarkable learning power of very young infants. Hand in hand with this capacity to learn by imitation and by exploration, the brain is growing rapidly. Its growth and development are likely to be the result of a complicated interaction between the child and its environment. The brain cells of the kittens mentioned in Chapter 1 became tuned to the kind of visual environment they had been brought up in and it is likely that our own brain's ability to interpret images and sounds does not develop to a precisely-designed blueprint but is modified physically by what is seen, heard and touched. These straws in the wind from brain research tell us that the quality of the environment – be it language, experiences of seeing, touching, smelling, explaining etc. – may influence the wiring patterns – the nerve pathways – of the young and growing brain.

A baby's active brain
We saw in the last chapter that a baby is born with a brain poised to learn language. The baby's brain is active in seeing, feeling and hearing a few days after birth. He blinks his eyes to a sudden sound, closes his eyes to a bright light, and a crooning voice nearby will often stop him crying. But at one month his brain has matured sufficiently for him to fix on the most important parts of a familiar pattern, on the eyes in the mother's face. To him, at this time, her eyes probably have high black and white content and *move*. He directs his gaze on them as she feeds him or talks to him. He stops whimpering and usually turns towards the sound of a soothing voice. At three months colour vision is developing and red can be distinguished from yellow. By this time he is visually alert. Mother's entire face is smiled at, not just the eyes. He recognizes his feeding bottle and he makes eager welcoming movements as it comes near his face. Clearly the seeing (visual) parts of the brain are active in making sense of what he sees. At six months when he is left with a stranger, his face sobers and he may cry. This is because the memory and seeing parts of the brain have developed far enough to distinguish between 'mother' and an unfamiliar face.

All this suggests that the capabilities of the young brain unfold to an ordered timetable (see Figure 4 and Table 7, pages 65–8). What a baby 'sees' seems to be dependent upon the maturation of three networks of nerves in the brain: a primary visual system basic to the perception of a pattern like a whole face; a more primitive 'second' visual system limited to the detection of only the most salient elements in a pattern – the eyes in a face (the contours within and around the eye seem to rivet the infant's attention to this feature); and finally various nerve pathways in the brain controlling eye movements which enable a baby to track small moving objects like a toy moved in front of him or help him to gaze steadily at the fine detail of something in front of him, such as his fingers.

At birth and in the first few weeks of life what a baby sees seems to be mediated by the ancient (in the evolutionary sense) second system which remains in man as an adjunct to the more recently evolved primary system. Various parts of the mid-brain are involved in this second system which are covered by the new brain. As life progressed up the evolutionary ladder a sheet of cells began to develop from the front edge of the ancient brain and spread backwards over it like a cap; and indeed it is our thinking cap. This began to fold and crumple in an attempt to pack an ever increasing surface into the skull. This convoluted new brain is the cortex which perhaps analyses the visual message into its separate parts – shape, movement, colour, distance – but how the message is encoded and then unscrambled and where it is read is not known. Nevertheless the more sophisticated reactions that begin to appear in the second and third month of life reflect a dawning participation of the recently evolved 'primary' system in what a baby sees. He recognizes his feeding bottle (and therefore memory systems must be developing) and is preoccupied by a nearby human face.

The nerve pathways in the developing brain must make a baby's eyes move towards a sideways stimulus – a window with the sunshine playing through it; must allow him to follow a moving object with smooth turning of the eyes; must help him to hold a steady focus on a small detail like the fringes of his pram blanket as he plays with them and finally must allow him to over-ride all these stimuli to shift his attention to a selected object – for example, to follow his mother bringing a favourite toy.

The last two mechanisms depend very much on the maturation of the *primary* visual system and on the middle part of the retina of the eye (important for distinguishing detail). To focus on anything of

Figure 4 Maturation of children's abilities and their link with brain development (compare with Table 7 on p. 68)

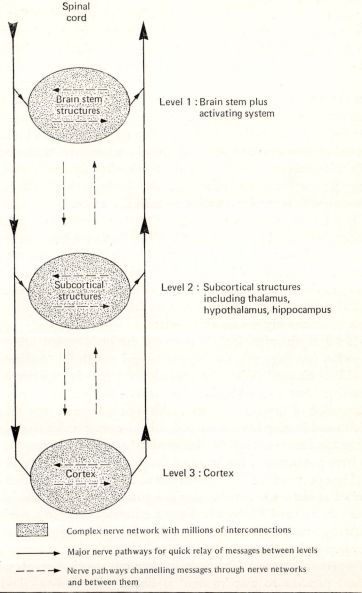

Spinal cord

Brain stem structures

Level 1 : Brain stem plus activating system

Subcortical structures

Level 2 : Subcortical structures including thalamus, hypothalamus, hippocampus

Cortex

Level 3 : Cortex

Complex nerve network with millions of interconnections

Major nerve pathways for quick relay of messages between levels

Nerve pathways channelling messages through nerve networks and between them

From Gordon Bronson 'Hierarchical organisation of the Central Nervous System', *Early Human Development.*

The brain has a timetable of development which depends upon the maturation of nerves. Thus a child's capacity to walk, to talk, to learn, to respond to stimulation, will all be determined by the maturity of particular nerve networks at particular ages. Premature babies reach speech milestones at about the same time as babies born at normal time and stand and walk no sooner.

Level 1 structures in the diagram above (see also Figure 5, page 76) are operational at birth and are controlled by the brain stem and 'activating' system to give vigorous but ineffectual squirming and kicking. The range of stimuli influencing the baby are: sudden loud sounds, bright lights. Some of the stimuli are internal to make a baby cry with hunger or pain. All these stimuli influence behaviour through simple brain structures. His brain is not sufficiently developed to recognize complex patterns like a face.

Level 2 and 3 structures gradually start to come into operation during the second and third month of life. By then a baby can begin to focus his attention on something (see page 65). In the second month the start of smiling in response to a face begins and shows that the visual areas and temporal lobes of the cortex have matured sufficiently to dimly encode important features of patterns like the eyes in a face – but not yet a whole face.

Level 2 structures include parts of the brain which influence emotion (see page 78). During the second month the 'undifferentiated continuum' of a baby expands to a growing spectrum of emotional states – gratification, frustration – and possibly shows the maturation of Level 2 structures. Although at three months simple vision and hearing have developed, a baby cannot understand what he sees and hears because the 'interpretive' areas in the cortex (Level 3) have not matured. But by three months memories have built up and he can encode entire patterns: it is not just a pair of eyes that are smiled at but a whole face. Also one pattern can be distinguished from another and a baby can detect a mismatch between a familiar pattern (a face) and a strange one. So a fear of strangers begins to develop and the 'sobering' of the face when his mother leaves the room (at six months). The brain by then can associate events with visual patterns so that 'mother' is linked with feeding, singing nursery rhymes, smells and so on. As far as motor (physical) development is concerned, the upper part of the body and the arms lead, with the head and hand joining them at about six months. This level of maturation is mirrored in the motor and sensory parts of the cortex (Level 3). The leg areas of the cortex remain the least developed up to about two and do not catch up till three at the earliest.

After two, details of brain development are obscure but it is likely that maturation continues until adolescence. This must be the case in the development of Level 2 structures (the hypothalamus) since the trigger to begin adolescence is pulled when nerve tissue in the hypothalamus matures to cause the pituitary gland to function. Then the monthly waxing and waning tides of hormones are started in the female and in the male the nonrhythmic pattern. A glance at Table 7 will underline the impressive learning abilities of a child of three. Of course all children are unique and develop at different rates. The milestones in the table are only average ones. Though we know only a little about the brain we need to use what information we have about its growth and maturation and to try to recognize in a child how ripe he is to learn a particular concept.

Table 7 Maturation of children's abilities*

Time	Motor Development	Cries and Language
Birth	Reactions mainly reflex dependent on condition of baby – alert or drowsy.	Cries vigorous but variable in pitch, quality and duration.
4 weeks	Large jerky movements of limbs, arms more active than legs.	Cries lustily when hungry or in pain. Little guttural noises when content.
12 weeks	Lifts head. No grasp.	Smiles, coos, vowel-like sounds.
20 weeks	Grasps, sits with props.	Consonantal sounds, labial fricatives, spirants, and nasals.
6 months	Sits. Stands only with support.	Babbling. One syllable utterances, 'ma', 'da', 'di'.
10 months	Creeps, pulls to standing position.	Sound play, gurgling, imitates. Differentiated responses to words heard.
12 months	Walks when hand held. Crawls on feet and hands. Sits on floor. Picks up sweet between finger and thumb.	Definite single words, 'mamma', 'dadda'. Definite understanding of simple commands.
18 months	Walks alone. Sits on chair. Builds tower with 3 cubes (hard). Scribbles with crayon.	Has repertoire of 3–50 word items, used singly. No frustration if not understood.
24 months	Runs, walks up and down stairs. Unwraps sweets efficiently.	Vocabulary more than 50 words. Two-word phrases.
30 months	Jumps, stands on one foot. Builds tower of 6 cubes. Pushes and pulls large toys skilfully but not good at steering. Holds pencil in preferred hand.	Vocabulary increasing very fast. Utterances of 2, 3, and even 5 words. Grammar not always understandable. Seems to understand everything said to him. Frustrated if not understood.
3 years	Runs, operates tricycle. Draws a man with head. Copies circle and cross. Cuts with scissors.	Vocabulary of 1,000 words. Grammar complex essentially adult and understandable.
4 years	Jumps over rope, catches ball, walks a line. Builds tower of 10 + cubes. Draws a man with head, legs, trunk and usually arms and fingers.	Language differs from adult only in style rather than grammar.
5 years	Active and skilful in climbing, sliding, swinging, digging. Dances to music. Plays a variety of ball games with great ability. Grips strongly with either hand.	Speech fluent and grammatical. Loves stories and acts them out in detail later, alone or with friends. Enjoys jokes and riddles. Can give name and age and often birthday. Gives home address.

* These time-markers are only a rough guide. There is enormous variation in patterns of development.

acquired interest (like a feeding bottle or a favourite toy) the baby must be guided by memory systems developing in the temporal cortex (see page 79). Precise movements of the eye to keep it fixed accurately on small details also seem to be dependent on the development of 'feature-detecting' cells (see page 80) in the visual cortex. The automatic shifting of the eyes towards a peripheral stimulus and the smooth following of an object seem to be controlled by midbrain structures of the *second* visual system in response to information coming in from the sides of the retina (which mature before the central part) referred to above. So we can say that nerve-fibres from the eyes go not only to the visual cortex (the primary system) but also to a mid-brain structure (the second system) called the 'superior colliculus', a pair of bumps on the back of the brain stem which connects the cerebral hemispheres to the spinal cord. It may be that the two visual systems in the brain are the 'where' system in the colliculus and the 'what' system in the cortex. Not surprisingly the 'where' system is involved in the control of eye movements. Perhaps the colliculus may be involved in determining whether objects are important and speeding up the eye movements if necessary.

The reason for going into this amount of detail is to emphasize what an infant is 'seeing'; just how much it can learn from anything it sees must be very dependent upon the stage the developing brain has reached. But by six months a baby is visually alert and its memory systems are developing rapidly.

Not irrelevant to visual alertness, and its development, is the need to pick up a baby when he cries. Not only does he stop crying but he frequently becomes visually alert and scans the surroundings. If regular soothing of this nature makes him alert (as seems likely) it follows that a baby picked up for crying will have earlier and more opportunities to explore his mother – face, smell, touch – than babies left crying in the cot or pram. So don't underestimate a baby and don't leave a baby crying because you think it is bad for him to be picked up.

A child may even be able to reason before one. It seems likely that when something vanishes behind a screen, a one-year-old knows that it is still there even if he can't see it.

This remarkable capacity of the baby and young child to learn disturbs some of the theories of the past. It was held by Jean Piaget that not until seven or eight does a child develop powers of logical analysis which enable him to infer that if one thing is bigger than a second, and the second is larger than the third, then the first must be bigger than the third. But children of four seem to be able to think logically so long as they can remember the crucial steps in an argument.

And most important is a child's gradual development of more subtle aspects of human behaviour like the growth of moral judgment. Any parent or teacher will recognize how a child of six or seven knows that it is wrong to steal, to tell lies, to cry for nothing and to fight. Then he will not be ripe to understand social injustice. By nine to twelve he will know the injustice of 'a mother who won't allow her children to play with children who are less well dressed', or a teacher who prefers a pupil because he is stronger, or cleverer or better dressed.

Of course, children differ remarkably in the way they unfold physically, mentally and emotionally. Each child goes through the same order of development but at different rates. Each of us is different and develops in a flexible, dynamic way, responding to this or that influence; and next to the parent, the teacher is probably the greatest influence on a child.

Work equals play

The learning capacity which a child's rapidly developing brain gives him is truly remarkable. Here is Niko Tinbergen's (1975) description of exploratory learning in a three-year-old – experimenting, ordering his thoughts, pretending. It will ring true to any mother of a toddler:

> It discovers more and more; it finds out what it can do with things; it constructs, for instance, when playing with blocks and even with sand, mud, leaves. In the process, it also develops its imaginativeness, for instance, when it treats a rag or a soother as a friend: when it handles and speaks to say, a hot-waterbottle as to another being – in general, when it plays pretend games. It even experiments, and so learns the essentials of cause-effect relationships (beating with your spoon on a table produces a funny sound) and it simply loves to make jokes (a carefully built tower

of blocks is suddenly knocked over, with obvious glee). The variety, richness and growth of exploratory play is almost without limits and for the observant child watcher there is never a dull moment. And all the time the child categorises and in general orders its thoughts. An underfive may already have discovered some elements of arithmetic, and it also begins to play with language.

And to jump two years, here is what some five-year-olds learned by discovery play with bricks. They had been taken to see a bridge by their teacher (Archer):

> The children returned to school and wanted to build a bridge 'just like the one we have seen'. After much trial and error and repetitive play for several days they were able to produce an interesting group of bridges spanning various kinds of roadways and intersections.

By feeling, seeing, and using the different types of brick they experienced roughness, smoothness, heaviness and lightness. They were encouraged to use correct words, the play and situation creating the *need* for the language; 'concrete', 'brick', 'strong', 'arch', 'dump-truck'. Discussion went on about 'what kind of traffic goes over the bridge'. And incidentally they learned a great deal about science and mathematics through sensing the effect of gravity and sorting and ordering the various shapes and sizes of block.

A child does not only explore in this fashion. He has developed a great capacity for *imitating*, that is, translating perceived into performed movements. At eighteen months, for example, a child 'reads' a book, brushes the floor and kisses a doll in imitation of his mother. Perhaps this was one of the most important steps in the development of his brain. Most young children love to help mother or father dust and sweep and polish and cook, or to work in the garden, bash the typewriter, or put up a shelf. What they have learnt is seen in children 'playing out' the activity they have been closely observing, be it mother or father or the milkman, or the driver of the digger outside. And as they play so language develops, more vividly according to what they see and how much the parents praise and encourage experiment and talk about it, even though it is messy, noisy and destructive.

One interesting discovery about language development in boys and girls aged eighteen months to three and a half concerns the different settings in which they are involved in talk. Boys talk more when playing alone while girls speak more when eating, playing with or helping other children. The origin of these differences seems to be the context in which parents choose to initiate conversation. Most of the conversations started with girls are during helping and 'nonplay' activities. With boys most conversation has a play setting. From a very early age mothers associate their daughters with domestic chores rather than their sons! But what really matters in talk linked with play or helping about the house is the *effort* a parent makes in trying to understand a child's meaning and to help him to express himself coherently rather than dismissing a jumble of words as nonsense. Children who have had this sort of cooperation make good listeners and talkers at school.

The essential theme in all these examples is the astonishing capacity of the child to learn early by imitation, by imaginative and discovery play and domestic play. His brain is ready for it. The practical point is not to bore a baby or young child by making him sit in his cot or pram for long hours or penning him in a room with nothing to do. It may give a mother more freedom but her child is not using his brain and a baby will simply sleep for lack of anything to see. Time and patience are essential.

The illustrations serve to underline other points. Children need security at play. They need to know that mother is not too far away. Parents need to know when to join in and when to hold back. Too much joining in, and too much taking the lead can hamper, even kill, learning by play. In fact, conversation by children often stops when an adult approaches. But if an adult is sensitive, children's play can be enhanced and a suggestion may prevent play reaching stalemate and becoming repetitive. Adults need to have a role in children's play, but a subtle one.

Needs of children
In organized conditions like a playgroup, nursery class and primary school perhaps each child's needs should be analysed very carefully

so that individual needs in play and language can be met. Some children get plenty of talk, books, visits and problem-solving activities but perhaps not all that much rough and tumble play. Other children rove the streets. They are certainly not short of language experience or group play but need a one-to-one interaction with an adult who not only supplies words and ideas but also experiences from which language arises like those mentioned in Chapter 4. Children from rowdy homes may need quiet spaces and a teacher who will help with things the mother has not managed to do with them. Many town children need to see, feel and smell, living and growing things. Such experiences will help the mind to grow.

References

ARCHER, H. Personal communication with author but see also PARRY, M. and ARCHER, H. (1973) *Preschool Education* Macmillan
BRAIN, W. R. (1960) *Mind, Perception and Science* Oxford University Press
TINBERGEN, N. (1972) Functional ethology and the human sciences *Proc. R. Soc. B.* 182
TINBERGEN, N. (1975) The importance of being playful *Times Educational Supplement* January

Chapter 6

Learning: how the brain predicts

The ability to forecast must be tied up with the evolution of the human brain. One of the mysteries of evolution is the brain's explosive growth during the late Pleistocene era. Perhaps the ability to predict – not only by logic but by intuition and imagination, and to keenly observe – developed strongly then so that physically the mysterious grey matter came to provide the organ of thought.

So far we have considered feeding information and experience to the young, growing brain. The brain receives and then predicts. In a way the sense organs are rather like instruments collecting information which is then ordered by the brain into hunches which can be tested out by further investigation, just like the baby with the thistle. To put it very crudely, the child's brain is developing the power to predict what might happen if he did so and so. It is almost as if small-scale experiments go on inside the head which link new information pouring in from the senses with what has been learned previously and stored away in the memory. If experience says 'go on' or 'stop' or 'test further' this action follows.

This capacity to *predict* is the key to human success. The human brain in its predicting power is not like a slot machine where an answer comes out yes or no. It is a very flexible machine which seems to work towards its answers by running through a series of memory sequences which are something like the particular situation. 'Is that a friendly dog?' the brain says, and this experience of a particular dog is weighed up against past experiences of dogs in general and perhaps the child may laugh and want to stroke it or run away in tears, depending on experience.

To make predictions a memory store is necessary which can be consulted when presented with a particular situation. This memory store can be thought of rather crudely as a 'model of the world' which is physically located in the brain. We are so familiar with this model or picture that we think it *is* the outside world.

The model is a highly personal one because it is made up from information which is *selected*. That is, in our daily lives and from childhood, we tend to ignore some things and emphasize others. But the whole aim of learning is to provide a brain model which is useful in helping to predict the future: what might happen if . . . ? Clearly the model becomes richer and more useful with experience. When people have been blind from birth and their blindness is cured, they see nothing but confused images which they are not able to identify. These people gradually learn by trial and error to make a practical model.

A brain alphabet

What is the physical basis of this model? Is it made out of anything in the head? It is possible that it is assembled out of units which are inherited and which must be in the brain. These basic units, which may be compared with a ready-made alphabet, may be in real terms the cells of the brain, which are capable of keeping account of events and remembering things in almost unlimited number. These cells are not all the same and their particular character is given to them by the receiving gear in each cell. This is formed by thin branching tendrils, the dendrites mentioned previously; some cells have few unbranched dendrites and others have many, and thus it is possible that the differing shapes of the dendrites form the 'memory alphabet'. In animals such as the guinea pig, the cat and the mouse, the dendritic patterns are fixed very early, sometimes at birth. In man they may be fixed but it is more likely perhaps that the dendrites can to some extent respond – that is alter in shape – to experiences during a life-time. Sir John Eccles (1965), a great neurologist, believes that the richness of human performance stems from the potentiality of the human cerebral cortex for developing subtle and complex nerve webs of the utmost variety, a potentiality perhaps not shared by even the most intelligent animal.

The basic requirement of a dendrite alphabet is that it is a suitable one to store representations of all the situations an animal is likely to meet in a lifetime. Evidence from experiments on the frog's eye shows that its 'visual alphabet' is simple and allows storage of infor-

Figure 5   A diagram of the human brain

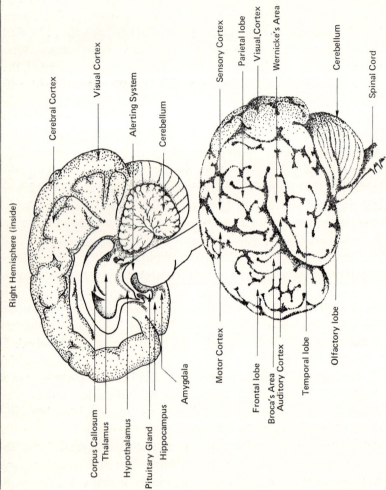

Right Hemisphere (inside)

Cerebral Cortex

Visual Cortex

Alerting System

Cerebellum

Corpus Callosum
Thalamus

Hypothalamus

Pituitary Gland
Hippocampus

Amygdala

Sensory Cortex

Parietal lobe

Visual Cortex

Wernicke's Area

Cerebellum

Spinal Cord

Motor Cortex

Frontal lobe

Broca's Area
Auditory Cortex

Temporal lobe

Olfactory lobe

Left Hemisphere (surface)

Cerebral Cortex Grey matter covering surface of cerebral hemispheres, 3–4 millimetres thick.

Motor Cortex A strip of cortex which controls specific muscle acts organized by the whole cortex.

Sensory Cortex A strip of cortex which receives 'sensations' from the skin.

Auditory Cortex Area of cortex in temporal lobe. Receives reports of auditory sensation.

Olfactory Lobe The smell brain. In man visual clues are more important than smell but particular smells may suddenly arouse visual and other memories.

Visual Cortex Area of cortex at the rear of each hemisphere which receives reports of visual sensation via the thalamus.

Parietal Lobe Seems to control relationship between body and mind. Injuries can disturb knowledge of where parts of the body are.

Frontal Lobe 'Silent' areas (electrical stimulation does not lead to movement). Probably concerned with inhibition, to make man pursue activities and investigation in a restrained and orderly way.

Temporal Lobe Together with the hippocampi plays a crucial role in remembering.

Broca's Area Controls speech. Damage causes any speech that remains to be curt, telegraphic and laborious.

Wernicke's Area May be involved in the understanding and analysis of speech.

Corpus Callosum An enormous strip of millions of nerves which link the two halves of the brain.

Thalamus A relay station for sensory messages to the cortex, said to give emotional tone to cortical experience.

Hypothalamus The supreme regulator of instinctive behaviour (thirst, aggression, sex). Works through pituitary and nervous system.

Pituitary Gland Master gland of the body largely controlled by hypothalamus.

Hippocampus Tucked inside the temporal lobes. Important in laying down or retrieving long-term memories.

Amygdala Part of the 'old' brain which regulates instinctive (perhaps aggressive) behaviour.

Alerting System Large untidy tangle of nerves possibly important in the maintenance of consciousness.

Cerebellum The automatic pilot of the brain which organizes complex muscle teamwork.

Spinal Cord The slender part of the central nervous system extending from the brain down the back. The backbone surrounds and protects the cord.

The brain of a normal adult weighs on average about 1,300 grams. Brain weight is not necessarily correlated with ability but the cut-off seems to come in adults below 1,200 grams. The cortex forms a layer of grey matter 3 millimetres thick. If it could be unfolded and spread out it would form a sheet of about 2,000 square centimetres. In a real brain, as opposed to a diagram, the sensory, motor and thinking parts of the cortex are not neatly arranged in order but are intermingled, though in order. Imagine a shirt hung out on a line to dry and the same article screwed up in a ball in the washing machine: the parts of the shirt are still in the same order as are the parts of the cortex. Diagrams too imply that the functions of the brain are specifically localized. Francis Gall (1758–1828), the brain anatomist, suggested that personality characteristics were located in various parts of the cortex. It was a reasonable guess and no more silly than that of Descartes who located reason in a pea-sized gland, the pineal, whose true function is still uncertain. Although brain functions are largely localized, they have many alternative channels available to them so that destruction of one pathway does not abolish the functions. The 'emotional' centres of the brain (the amygdala and hypothalamus) are deep in the middle but have rich connections with the frontal, 'thinking' centres. This merely serves to illustrate that thinking involves many different parts of the brain; rational thought is tinged with varying degrees of emotion. Every living brain is unique and its wiring patterns differ from every other brain.

mation that is likely to be of interest to the frog. Its visual alphabet might consist of only six 'letters' which can code experiences such as tracking moving insects or jumping towards blue rather than other colours (frogs jump towards open water rather than towards vegetation). Our own visual alphabet must be a good deal more complicated than this.

The cortex (or grey matter) where this brain alphabet is likely to be, is a double structure, tightly folded to pack in an enormous surface area (see Figure 5, pages 76–7). Each half or hemisphere of the cortex is similar in structure and the halves are joined by rich nerve connections. Each half has a kind of lobe on it like the thumb of a boxing glove beside the fist. This is the temporal lobe. Tucked inside each lobe is a twisted structure, like a seahorse, the hippocampus. It is possible that the temporal lobes and the hippocampi together play a crucial role in memory. Perhaps the temporal cortex is like a complicated filing cabinet and the hippocampus is the key which unlocks it and makes available a 'strip' of past experience in complete detail from the brain cortex as fresh and vivid as when it was first recorded. I have said 'perhaps' and 'possible' because the mechanism of memory is still obscure. Hard evidence does suggest, though, that the temporal lobes have a key part in memory. (Gentle electrical stimulation of the temporal lobes of a patient before brain surgery has made the patient experience a 'flashback' of the past.) The role of the hippocampus in memory, however, is still controversial.

In normal life perhaps the hippocampus-temporal lobes might act to scan new information coming into the brain from the eyes, fingers, nose, ears. The brain inspects it to see whether it is familiar by making available past memories with which the new experience can be matched and interpreted. What the brain then tells us to do depends on the model. A child makes progressive additions to, or changes in, the model. If an event proves to be extremely significant he may remember it for the rest of his life; if not the memory fades in a day or two. In other words a child chooses from what he sees and hears: that which is significant is remembered, that which is not is forgotten quickly. Every time he sees a dog to which he pays attention he modifies his 'model' of a dog in the brain.

Here is a description of an encounter between a spider and a child.

I expect all of us have had similar experiences but might not be able to express them as vividly as Margaret Lane does:

> My feelings towards spiders have drastically changed since I was a small child. I was first taught by a silly nurse to fear them, and when she once commanded me to capture a spider in the bath with a piece of paper, and the creature squashed to pulp under my fingers, I went into horror-shock which lasted for decades. But a very long time afterwards, living in an old house in the west of Ireland, I became fascinated by a huge spider-web which was every day spun in an outside corner of my deep window.
>
> Every day the well-meaning daily with duster slashed at the web and destroyed it, and every morning it would be found flawlessly spun and stretched anew, the spider sitting alert in a corner cranny, one foot on the communication-cord, waiting for the signal that would tell her that some luckless fly had floundered into her meshes. The spider herself was very handsome, large and plump with a back as boldly marked as a tabby-cat's. I arranged for her not to be disturbed, and became addicted. Soon I was catching flies for her benefit and dropping them lightly into the shining web, entranced to see how quickly she ran to the prize, wrapped it up swiftly in silken threads whipped out of her hindquarters and hung it from the stone ceiling of the window-frame, where she kept a larder of what looked like miniature cellophane-wrapped hams.

I said earlier that the model must be assembled out of units in the brain – the cells of the cortex. It is very unlikely that the brain contains special cells that are keyed to react to a face or to a hand. This would lead to push-button 'either/or' responses like the frog's responses mentioned. Rather the cortex contains cells which react to *broad* classes of stimuli: amount of contour, size, movement, receding or approaching objects. All the time the brain seems to be searching for meaningful combinations of features which define the boundaries of a pattern like a face or a scene, but it is quite unclear how the brain's classifying cells, the 'alphabet' works. The output from these cells is encoded and stored (but how is obscure) so that it can be used as described previously to scan new data entering the brain through the senses.

A model of 'mother'

The idea of the model can be applied with particular relevance to the baby's developing appreciation of his mother or her substitute. When a baby is born he has no experience. He has to start with something. It might be an inborn pattern of feature-detecting cells previously described, which respond to a face which incorporates all the appropriate clues that the brain analyses into a pattern. The baby smiles and his pleasure is reinforced by food and warmth so a face-pleasure-food link is formed. These nerve links have, at first, high 'thresholds' but with continual use become a nerve web. The face has now turned into 'mother' with her smile, warmth, scent, the songs she sings, and food. The webs are called 'engrams' – a kind of writing left behind in the brain by conscious experience – built up through nerve connections in the cortex, by learning.

As the brain matures it becomes more discriminating. At three months, the model of his mother is not at all clear and a baby smiles happily at anyone. But by six months the temporal lobes and the visual areas of the brain have matured sufficiently to distinguish one pattern from another. Then the uncertainty about strangers begins because of a mismatch between the model he has built up of familiar persons and strangers.

By three the brain has matured far enough for a child to know that mother will be 'back later'. He can talk and understand past and present. But mother must be back or the model will be confused, a child's predictions will become uncertain, and his confidence wane.

Some of the fears of childhood can be explained by the immaturity of the model. A child may think that because his grandpa died a week ago, his mother or father, because they are grown up, might die soon and he may nurse a worry. His parents may quarrel violently and his mother threaten to run away or kill herself. Even though those threats are out of character and are quickly forgotten, the child does not know this. His brain worries and he is unable to set the worry into an adequate context.

John Bowlby, the psychiatrist, believes that certain school phobias can be explained on these grounds: the child is not frightened of school but feels, and with good reason, insecure about *home*. So he wants to go back home to make sure all is well. Here are a few examples of 'school phobia' reported by John Bowlby (1973).

Clearly bullying boys, unkind teachers and bad health are all regarded as villains of the piece when a child is frightened of school. And it is a reasonable, if superficial, supposition. As a rule such children are well-behaved, anxious and inhibited. Most have good homes and parents who are worried about their refusal to go to school. Sometimes relations between child and parent are suffocatingly close.

If looked at more closely the home situation shows a mother, or more rarely a father, who is a sufferer from chronic anxiety and wants the child to stay at home for company. Or the child himself feels that his mother or father might drop dead or run away or commit suicide and so remains at home to prevent it happening. Sometimes a child fears that he might die or become ill if he is away from home. Sometimes, too, the mother, or more rarely the father, fears that something dreadful will happen to the child while he is at school and so keeps him at home.

None of these situations is terribly obvious and only comes out by hints. A boy of ten for example told a doctor 'very confidentially' that one reason for his occasional reluctance to go to school was his dislike of leaving his mother alone as 'it was just possible that she might run away'. It is very likely that the mother had made just that threat.

Another boy on hearing music that reminded him of the funeral of a neighbour who had committed suicide while her child was at school, suddenly felt 'funny' and had an irresistible urge to see his mother. The interpretation by the person listening was vague. John Bowlby writes, 'Let a spade be called a spade: it seems more likely that Peter had heard his mother threaten suicide.'

Remembering

But returning to memory, what is the fine basis of remembering a face or a voice or the complete model? How is it stored and how is it turned from the stored material, whatever it is, into the picture of a face or a scene in the mind?

One theory is that remembering consists of the manufacture of specific chemical molecules in the brain, each molecule tailor-made to a particular memory. Thus when we think back to that particular experience, the chemical code must 'somehow' give up its memories in all their colour and sound and then return them to their stored condition.

To crack the problem of memory, and therefore the brain model, will be tough. It is clear that we have hardly scratched the surface. But whatever theories are advanced they must be compatible with two commonsense observations:

1 The brain works (almost) as a unit. This is shown by the impossibility of speaking effectively while reading, writing and listening. In other words the brain seems to work as one central coordinating register or dictionary rather than from bits of information filed here and there. But I said 'almost' because it is not impossible to do two things at once. Some people talk or whistle while driving quite skilfully!

2 Memory thrives on 'associations'. Say a word – 'moon' for instance – and at once a collection of memories and associations are summoned up.

Where learning is concerned, three points are worth making:

1 The most basic thing that can be said about memory, after a century of intensive research, is that unless detail is placed into a structured pattern, it is rapidly forgotten. In other words, if the material to be recalled is unrelated, such as a string of random numbers, a child will remember much less than if the material is connected as in a story or sentence.

2 A child may learn or is capable of remembering only those things to which he pays *attention*. None of the things he ignores leaves a memory trace in the brain. Only when a child is focusing his attention on something is he writing on the brain's slate. So what is 'relevant' and interesting to a child is likely to be remembered perhaps for the rest of his life. That which he cannot relate to life or later to job-expectation, or which has little meaning or significance to him, is likely to be forgotten rapidly.

3 Anxiety can reduce the brain's capabilities, including concentration and memory. Anxiety has many root causes. For the child at school it may lead to school phobia as already described.

To summarise: whatever physical base for memory exists in the brain the model of the world created in the brain cells must depend on the quality of experience a child gains through his sensory system. Indeed, the whole purpose of learning is to improve our model of the world so that we can make useful forecasts. This description of how the young brain learns to make 'forecasts' does not mean that decisions to do and say things are made entirely by cold reason. Human beings are not cold calculators. Decision by a child of say, twelve can include logic. But it can be based on hunch, gut reaction and imagination. It is not possible to give easy prescriptions for helping a child to develop a good model because each family, like its individual members, is unique. Attitudes to play, work, discipline, success and happiness, may vary, but every small child needs a mother or father or another loved person to give unhurried attention and to provide a consistent, caring, continual model in his world.

References

BOWLBY, J. (1973) *Separation, Anxiety and Anger* Hogarth Press

ECCLES, J. (1965) *The Brain and the Unity of Conscious Experience* Cambridge University Press

LANE, M. (1977) Learning to love spiders *Daily Telegraph* May 7th

Chapter 7

Learning: left and right hemispheres

A major point of emphasis in this book has been that the young brain is plastic – changeable, flexible, in fact, 'open' to learning. This flexibility coupled with the rapid growth of the brain but slow growth of the body up to puberty gives man a 'long childhood' in which to learn from others.

The higher and lower brain

The cortex is the enormous sheet of grey matter we use when we think. It is a double structure with each half or hemisphere connected. Some parts of the cortex have a specific job to do and if any of the special parts is damaged, the corresponding ability is impaired. An accident to the back of the head, which affects the visual cortex which somehow turns what we see by way of the eye into a three-dimensional world in all its colour and brightness, may cause total or partial blindness. And, as I have said earlier, one hemisphere of the cortex, usually the left, is detailed to handle the problems of speech.

Besides the cortex, which is largely taken up with 'higher' abilities like speech and thought, and the power to predict and reason out a situation, there are more primitive or 'lower' areas buried deep in the centre of the brain and overlain by the great convoluted sheet of grey matter.

These lower regions seem to provide the springs of life, urging us on to act as we do. There are regions of the brain where injuries produce either excessive eating or refusal to eat, whereas other parts promote sexuality and sleeping and waking and so on. Some of these actions are assisted by hormones, chemicals secreted into the blood under the control of the brain.

There is little doubt that the actions of these regions of the brain play a big part in providing the motivations, sometimes called the drives, to act in particular ways. The relation of these to our subjective feelings, desires, choices and intentions, is very difficult to decide. New knowledge has here outstripped our capacity to talk sensibly about it. But there is little doubt that most of our feelings and even decisions are at least strongly influenced by these parts of the brain and add emotional drive to the logical activities of the grey matter which might otherwise be cold.

Besides the cortex and the inner core of the brain, there is the cerebellum and the bulb (see Figure 5, page 76). The cerebellum, which is a kind of automatic pilot, lies below the back of the cortex. It can take over actions merely sketched out by our conscious minds and arrange complex muscle teamwork to bring the actions about. This leaves the mind free at the same time to get on with the job of thinking and creating. Thus a child can ride his bike to school solving the previous night's maths homework before the lesson.

The bulb which continues the spinal cord into the skull, contains the centres for life and death functions like breathing and the control of the tone of the blood vessels. Possibly it contains mechanisms which pick out the new and the interesting while suppressing the less important at a particular moment in time. You might sleep through the roar of motorbikes or rock music but wake to the baby's cry.

I have, in a way, compartmentalized the brain. But it does *not* work in sections. There are probably no set areas responsible for higher thinking like problem-solving or writing poetry. The brain seems to work as one unit and thinking and feeling go on throughout the brain whenever necessary.

The fuel of the mind
It should be clear by now that despite our present knowledge the brain is still like a map of Africa in 1850, two-thirds uncharted, and the other map references variable in accuracy.

For all its work the brain is not extravagant in its fuel requirements. The fuels for our thoughts are glucose at the rate of one teaspoonful an hour and oxygen at 46 millilitres a minute. The visual areas at the back of the brain are hungry for oxygen and use one-quarter of the brain's supply. If the circulation to the brain starts to fail, carbon dioxide will accumulate and cloud our thoughts. The breakdown of glucose by oxygen yields 20 watts, the electricity needed to light a dim bulb.

Our two brains

Although we are still at an early stage in understanding and mapping the brain, we do know something of practical importance to learning: the left and right hemispheres have different functions. The left talks, writes, does mathematics, and is logical. The right side recognizes patterns such as faces, is better in the construction of block designs and copying diagrams, is emotional, recognizes tunes, likes music, and is intuitive.

The two hemispheres do not work in isolation but are connected by an enormous strap which allows a two-way transfer of information along its millions of nerve fibres so that the two halves can share in memory and learning. The form in which information is transmitted is unknown, as are the details about which nerve paths are essential to the performance of particular tasks. Nevertheless, the interaction of the two hemispheres ensures that a fine balance is maintained between the abilities of each so that at the required moment one pan of the scales is raised and the other lowered. This fine balance ensures efficient mental activity. If the left hemisphere is inhibited (and it is not known how this damping works) the activity of the right increases perhaps to give full reign to the imagination or, more practically, to size up distance and objects to avoid an accident.

Reading and brain activity

To read and understand the meaning of this page requires balance between the two hemispheres such as has just been described. The right hemisphere recognizes the position and sequence of words, and the clues to meaning given by the individual words are interpreted by the left hemisphere. When position and meaning are integrated by both halves of the brain the passage is understood.

When a child stumbles on a difficult word (in say translating a language) he is likely to stick on that word rather than let his eyes rove a little way ahead to try to gain clues to meaning from the rest of the passage. If his eyes move from the word to scan ahead he might lose his place and the spatial activity in recovering it might jam the work of the left hemisphere which is trying to integrate the clues to meaning. The old method of marking the difficult word by putting a finger on it, then letting the eyes rove for meaning clues, allows the eyes to come back to the finger without effort; finger and eye work closely together automatically, and the brain is not troubled in finding its place. The finger is a solid point of reference so that the brain can explore meaning. The brain here is acting like a walker who is lost and pauses by some known spot, marked on his map, and decides from a survey of the terrain ahead which way to go. He is thinking and integrating clues but his position is fixed.

When a good reader tackles a difficult book, such as a foreign novel, he automatically breaks down difficult passages into manageable chunks, perhaps by right hemisphere activity. The pauses in between the chunks help him to think about the author's meaning by using his left hemisphere. A child or a poor adult reader, overconcentrating on individual words, tends to miss the overall meaning of a passage since perhaps overactivity on one side of the brain blocks activity on the other side, though this is only speculation.

At a certain stage a child can make progress by practising recognition and pronunciation of individual words without attempting to grasp the general sense, but later he must be led to understand that the phrase and then the sentence, and even the passage, are in reality the units which communicate the story which the author sets out to tell. The teacher or parent can demonstrate this by reading the story aloud. Clearly, some children grasp the need to scan ahead in larger units more readily than others, but it is an essential step for every child. In this way the two halves of the brain work efficiently together to read and understand the passage.

Reading is very much an *active* skill in that a good reader, checks, scans ahead, looks back. However, the aim of this book is not to give reading instruction, rather to paint in some of the neurological background to help those who are teaching children to read. But remember that young children are *naturally* disposed to learn how to read. (Smith)

Dyslexia
While there are no hard neurological facts to go on, perhaps 'dyslexia' can be explained by lack of coordination between the two

hemispheres. The right hemisphere, as described, takes care of spatial abilities, while the left looks after verbal intelligence. In dyslexia the functioning of the two halves may be out of phase, rather like a badly-tuned radio. The effect, or at least with words, seems to be a kind of interference between verbal and spatial functioning in the brain so that problems arise in reading, spelling and sequencing of letters in a word or words in a sentence.

Alternatively it may be that the nerve cells have failed to branch out properly so that learning difficulties may be due to nonconnection. Chapter 1 went into this; but if nutrition is very poor from the time of conception to about two or three, or if there has been destruction of the nerve cells by shortage of oxygen in early foetal life, learning difficulties could arise by failure of branching of the nerve cells.

Dyslexia is, however, not an easy handicap to define. Children with reading difficulties usually have a number of problems which can be to do with sight, hearing, memory *and* their emotional state (especially depression), or any combination of these. Absence from school in the early years is yet another cause. And to show how complex the matter is, 10 per cent of children with reading difficulties show visuo-spatial disorders. Dyslexia thus can be confused with general backwardness – some cynics say it is a middle-class name for general slowness – but children with 'dyslexia' often have normal intelligence. More boys than girls are affected (4 : 1); some are gifted in music, art and engineering (right-side bias). But it is as if a light goes out when a child handicapped by this condition attempts to read and write. The brain does not seem able to fit the words together. So misspelt, jumbled sentences reach the paper. And when the child tries to read the letters make nonsense.

All this observational evidence may point to faulty coordination between left and right hemisphere, or faulty 'wiring' of the nerves in the brain or both. But whatever the cause, such a child needs to be given confidence and help with reading, especially in the crucial years from four or five to eight, when the brain is in a critical time for language (reading) development. Patient teaching in small groups is important. The child needs to understand that he has a problem which has been diagnosed and that he is being helped. Failure is a big part of dyslexic children's lives. Once a child knows he is in difficulties he often tries to cover up and kicks against authority. So often aggressive behaviour and withdrawal are linked with this condition. Finding the right teacher for such children is crucial and not always easy.

The 'blank slate'

The two hemispheres described are not specialized at birth. They form part of the 'blank slate' on which will be written the lessons of experience. The writing starts at birth and may only take place when the baby is awake and concentrating the spotlight of his attention on something.

With increasing age specialization of the hemispheres begins and the 'spheres of influence' become established at about the age of two. Usually the left, as mentioned earlier, is specialized for language, mathematics and abstract thinking and the right for nonverbal memory and emotions. In some children, however, the pattern is not clear-cut and the cerebral hemispheres do not seem to acquire a clear functional specialization.

Because the left hemisphere is usually associated with speech and abstract thinking it became known as the 'dominant' hemisphere, the right, the 'minor' or 'subdominant'. But this is an old fashioned view for, as we have seen, each hemisphere has its own specialized functions.

If a child is going to be right-handed he is likely to be setting up the speech mechanism in the left hemisphere; but this is not always clear-cut. In two-thirds of left-handed children speech is located in the left hemisphere, and in the remaining third in the right. In other words, some left-handers use the left side of the brain for language and a few right-handers use the right side of the brain for language. A 'dominant' side controlling language or hand skills operates through *both* sides of the brain so that in speaking both sides of the tongue, face, throat work together. Similarly information from the ears and eyes reaches both sides of the brain but is passed to the dominant side for language analysis.

Artists and thinkers

A child's heredity determines which side of the brain becomes dominant, left or right. Ivan Pavlov divided people into artists and thinkers. The artists, with active and powerful right hemispheres, grasp the wholeness of things as a living unit; the thinkers, with dominant left hemispheres, attempt to analyse reality into its parts and later seek to put the bits together and breathe life into them. Einstein with left-side bias had as a professed aim: 'perception of this world by thought, leaving out everything subjective'. Shelley summed up his view with appropriate right-side bias: 'Most of the errors of philosophers have arisen from considering the human being in a point of view too detailed and circumscribed. He is not (only) a moral and intellectual – but also, and preeminently, an imaginative being. . . .' Yet he revealed by what he wrote how truly analytical he was. People, ordinary and extraordinary, are not 'either/or'. A research chemist and a child need to use three-dimensional imagery sometimes in their 'thinking'. We can all recognize left-and right-hemisphere tendencies in ordinary adults and in children. The genius or gifted may have more powerful and active dominance but they are certainly not as sharply divided as Pavlov thought.

The need for balance in experience

In children it is important not to pamper one hemisphere to the neglect of the other. Just as the body needs a balanced diet to grow and keep healthy so, as brain research has confirmed, the brain needs a balance of experience in order to learn properly. Most things young children learn involve both sides of the brain collaborating quite naturally. Drawing, model-making and painting have a bias to right-side activity. Mathematics inclines to the left hemisphere but spatial maths involves the right. Reading uses both and so does science. Experiment and analysis is left-sided activity but understanding the shape of molecules, right-sided. Writing involves pattern and spacing (right side) and meaning (left side).

As children grow older and specialization increases it is perhaps easy to neglect the strengths of the right hemisphere and parents and teachers should be aware of this. There is discipline in dance, sculpture, painting, drawing, drama and music different from but equally as vigorous and precise as mathematics and physics. Drawing and painting demand close coordination between hand, eye and brain. Children of eight and nine need to start to master *skills* in art, even copying the excellent and observing the tiny detail as well as expressing themselves in large paintings. Some children in any case are drawn to the minute.

In painting, drawing and modelling, the eye is in command and as a child matures the eye is under moral pressure to reject the false and sentimental while the hand is under severe discipline to control line and colour. Art, music and drama are not some fringe activity but are central to balanced development and the brain would be half-starved without them. The artistic side of a child needs to be cherished. It was Picasso who said: 'When I was a child I could draw like Titian but it took me all my life to learn to draw like a child.' As we all know only too well, the freshness and honesty of a child's vision can vanish.

Brain development in girls and boys

In young children's activities, right- and left-hemisphere development shows up sometimes in the playgroup, nursery class or home. Among most children there is a difference between boys and girls in the *speed* of nerve development in the left and right hemispheres. The speech areas in the left hemisphere are slightly more advanced in girls of four years than in boys of the same age. Parallel with this the speech organs of girls are more advanced – they talk earlier than boys. In boys, on the other hand, the right hemisphere is more developed and their capacity for spatial work is better, even from the age of two. At about six in boys the right side is still advanced for spatial processing but in girls it is not so specialized and can even take over language function after damage to the left side. Consequently girls seem to have greater plasticity for a longer period than boys, perhaps up to thirteen.

These differences in brain development show up in the behaviour of girls between three and five who become increasingly adept in talk and are often occupied in activities like crayoning, cutting out, and plasticine work. If talk is poor at home in these formative years, girls may lose out because they are passing through these crucial years for language development. Most boys of the same age are actively exploring and experimenting but are not talking so much. If you watch children's reactions to a strange toy, boys and girls behave quite differently. The boy will tend to be exploratory, curious and testing. He will persist, silently, in finding out whether a lever goes forward or back. There will be little about the toy that he does not find out. The girl will tend to explore at first and then give up.

Girls tend to be 'good at faces'. Incredibly, it is said, they can distinguish faces in a photograph before the age of one. Boys are not so quick at recognition but are much more accurate in their response to geometric shapes.

It is perhaps too blunt to say that girls are scientists about people and boys about things because there is, of course, a shading between male and female. None the less, there is a grain of truth in the generalization. Girls are always asking, 'Why did she say that about me?' They make observations about people all the time; how he or she looks, behaves, dresses; how old he or she is. In fact, once girls become skilled at talking they use it as their main means of finding out about the world, while boys go on exploring and investigating for much longer.

The roots of boy and girl differences in science and mathematics and in verbal facility are complex and controversial. In part they are very likely to be hereditary and adaptive, forged by human evolution for a life in a different kind of world from our own. Not many thousands of years ago, so short a time as to be like the last few words on the page of human evolution, the male was the hunter. He needed to fight and hunt (for which he needed good spatial sense in direction finding), to be exploratory and protective. The female needed to bring up the young safely and transmit the culture and language. This kind of behaviour, however lightly sketched, is basic and in our genes. Though it may be an evolutionary left-over, as useless as the appendix, it persists. Our own culture strongly re-inforces the basic difference between males and females, so that when boys and girls come to school at five they have started to behave differently.

The foundations of maths and science

The preschool years are a formative time for laying the foundations of maths and science, not as well-defined topics but incidentally, along with all the other ideas. The foundations of both subjects are learned early, not just through talk, which is important, but mainly by doing and experimenting with occasional help from an adult. From this practical activity children, with some stage-managing, can begin to abstract some general scientific ideas from their play. They can begin, for instance, to *classify* or *sort* materials that float or sink and then go on to test whether objects brought from home float or sink. They can play with sand, *comparing* wet and dry, and filling buckets full and half-full, and comparing their weights. They can *share* the sand between, say, a group of four. They can experiment by planting mustard seeds on sand and clay and learn to see which group grows faster, how much water they need each day, and then go on to see whether light is important for growth by putting one group of seedlings in a cupboard and leaving another in the light.

This messy play is the start of mathematical and scientific thinking. Perhaps girls miss out because they are not so interested in this sort of play and are mainly learning about the world through talk as suggested earlier. Boys may make up their language deficiencies when they start school at five, but it may be harder for girls to catch up on the *experience* of playing and experimenting with an adult who knows what questions to ask and what materials to provide. We should certainly plan appropriate numerical and spatial experiences for all young children but encourage girls to be as active as boys.

The following example illustrates the different play interests of boys and girls that have just been described. Play concerned with weddings is always popular in school (Archer):

Within the first half-hour the book corner became a church. All the eight girls crowded into the corner dressed in lace and terylene skirts from the dressing-up trolley. All the coloured net headdresses were used, and old white net curtains were in great demand – gliding brides seemed to carpet the floor space with their 'trains'. Soon, all the flower vases were emptied of their contents as the flowers were made into bouquets. (The boys were occupied elsewhere, and showed no interest in the girls' activities, so there were no bridegrooms. Since all the girls wanted to be brides, there were no bridesmaids or other attendants.) The books in the Book and Scripture Corner quickly doubled for hymn books, and Michaela guided the girls through the 'service'.

Once the food appeared, things were different; the boys, who were completely disinterested until now, hovered over the table and asked if they could play. The food looked very realistic. Weddings and receptions went well, boys joining in now, until Martin and Paul bit the ends off two sausages and reduced Jane and Sarah to tears. Kevin cracked a piece of egg on toast, and Michaela banished the boys from the party saying that they were 'spoiling everything'. To make up for the upset, we asked if they would like to make some real cakes – boys included – and we were taken up on our offer.

The purpose of this chapter has been to try and show that left and right sides of the brain have different functions and that we need to remember this in teaching and learning. Both hemispheres interact through massive linking nerve networks, each complementing the abilities in the other. Sometimes the abilities of each are combined in reading, writing and mathematics. Sometimes one side is used more and the activity of the other is damped down. When you brake hard to avoid a dog, you shut off the left side and use the right to size up where the car behind and the cyclist beside you are to avoid an accident. When you read the newspaper before supper you use both hemispheres; and when you relax after coffee and listen to music, you use the right. Always there is a delicate balance and collaboration which adjusts to everyday needs.

In educating children, neither side should be neglected but there is a tendency in later school life for the left to be pampered and the right to be a little starved. Both boys and girls should have experiences which give plenty to talk about and encourage the aptitudes of both hemispheres to be used to the fullest extent. An intellect that knows only what it can express in words and numbers is parched. It carries with it the danger of losing touch with the solid reality of earth and body and a loss of understanding of the feelings of other human beings.

Reference
ARCHER, H. Personal communication with the author but see also
  PARRY, M. and ARCHER, H. (1973) *Preschool Education* Macmillan
SMITH, F. (1971) *Understanding Reading* Holt, Rinehart and Winston

Chapter 8

Individuals all

All that has been written in this book about talk, exploratory play, level of expectation, growth of the body and intellect, depends very much on the kind of family a child is reared in. The family environment is crucial in determining which and how much of the potentialities inherited from parents are fulfilled. We cannot easily apportion the extent to which a particular characteristic is inherited and how much is due to the environment, simply because heredity and environment interact and the proportion of each is unique to each individual. Blanket statistics about IQ or health are useful for planners but do not help the individual much.

Each one of us has been formed by a kind of genetic lottery. Each is but *one* of a vast number of possible children any of whom might have been conceived and born if a different sperm and egg had fused, each with its own set of genes. In other words, each individual child is unique from the moment of conception and each has different potentialities all determined by the genetic code carried on the chromosomes. How these potentialities will develop and indeed *whether* they will, depends on the environment.

Much controversy surrounds the inheritance of 'intelligence' and it is certain that an individual's intelligence is partly a consequence of his genes, as are most of his physical and anatomical characteristics. So far it has proved impossible to measure with any degree of conviction how great a contribution heredity makes. Research has suggested that the inherited part of IQ lies between 25 and 65 per cent. For much of the population of America and Western Europe it is probably about 50 per cent.

Certain types of subnormal intelligence do have a very simple genetical basis. Sufferers from mongolism have a mean IQ of 30–35 (the average IQ is 100) and these unfortunate children have an extra chromosome which affects not only intelligence but development and behaviour. Phenylketonuria is another abnormality due to a recessive gene. The ill-effects of both abnormalities can be helped greatly by special 'environments' (by a special diet for phenylketonuriac children) but the major cause of low intelligence is heredity.

Normal intelligence (as measured by tests) is a graded character, like height, in which intermediate values in a large population are most common. It is not sharp and clear-cut like the possession of a particular blood group; it depends on the interplay of many 'plus' or 'minus' genes (each of which has a small quantitative effect on 'intelligence'), with many environmental factors which include conditions in the womb before a child is born. When a mother is bearing twins, food does not reach each twin equally and the smaller twin almost always has a slightly lower IQ. With these subtle, graded characters like IQ and height, it is very difficult indeed to unravel and separate the threads of heredity and environment.

The contributions of heredity and environment to a certain character, trait or disease may change with circumstances. Children, as we have seen, are now much taller than their counterparts at the turn of the century and this is the result of environmental improvements, not heredity. The same argument applies to the IQ and reading scores of children of West Indian parents born here and those born abroad. It is likely that advantages in schooling and upbringing cause the differences, not heredity.

There is no doubt then that the type of environment plays a big part in the way natural ability finds expression in children. Equally certain is the fact that heredity sets a limit to what each child can achieve in the best circumstances. No one doubts the truth of this when talking about footballers, ballet dancers and musicians, and it is equally true that a child with a low IQ will never make a nuclear physicist. But it is a *gross* oversimplification to say that people 'respond' to their environment like a plant thrusting to the light. Most of us live in environments that have been created for us by our own type; most gravitate instinctively towards an environment that suits body and mind. Temperamentally, that is *genetically*, different children elicit different behaviour from people. It is not a passive affair. Highly active babies and infants get more attention. They are less affected by a poor environment than passive infants simply because they demand and get more talk, more play and so on. 'Difficult' children seem to induce a hostile environment – perhaps because their very difficulty produces negative feelings in parents. Heredity and environment interact dynamically.

We should not assume, though, that heredity is soft. It can be very gritty. Witness your own family. Children who may tolerate each other's company at eight may well find it unbearable at eighteen and twenty-eight when their individual capacities have developed.

Without the genetic lottery mentioned earlier it would seem absurd to blame a conflict of parent and child on heredity. Yet even though that child has a better chance of being like his parents than anyone else in the world, the genetic individuality of the child overrides the parental environment. Heredity is hard. It takes all sorts to make a world, so the expression goes, and heredity sees to it that human individuality is maintained in all its wonder and delight.

But how does a parent or teacher cope, faced with an over-reactive, amoral, recalcitrant or gifted child – the spectacular individual? There is no easy formula to apply. Here is one example of a gifted child that might help, taken from Devon Education Department's (1977) report on gifted children. It shows individuality appearing early; how some of the boy's special needs were met and how he could have been thwarted into maladjustment. It shows heredity and environment interacting, yet heredity giving a vigorous and early push towards high ability.

Simon as a baby was slow and lethargic; he was very contented and almost a year old before he sat up. He made no attempt to crawl but played happily with whatever was within reach. Possible brain damage was suspected as a result of a long and difficult confinement. At fifteen months he just stood up and walked, and ran – properly, with no tottering or clinging.

As a toddler, his vocabulary was remarkable. He also showed a knowledge of colour at a very early age. His special ability (maths) was soon apparent. He knew, and appeared to understand, numbers very early.

At three to four years he still had an enormous vocabulary but could not be understood by many people as he had a tendency to say only the middle of words, not the beginning and end. He was tested at a clinic for possible deafness or speech defect. The clinic's conclusion was that nothing was wrong but that he was so quick and intelligent that his words couldn't keep pace with his thoughts. He had developed his own shorthand speech, which he knew his family understood.

When Simon went to his first primary school his progress in reading and especially in writing was very slow. It seemed that each day some topical sentences (which the children copied) were written on the board and then they added their own news and pictures. He had difficulty in transferring from blackboard to paper and rarely reached his own news and picture and became very bored. If he could have attempted his own news and picture first all might have been well.

Simon raced through number work and was outstanding orally. He showed virtually no interest in books and reading until about the age of eight, yet his general knowledge still increased fantastically. At about eight he started reading newspapers and discussing political and world events. He progressed to science fiction and then became an avid and fluent reader of fiction and nonfiction.

From the age of five, his love of maths was most apparent and he would spend long sessions in his bedroom working out things like how many seconds there are in a year. At the age of six years the family moved to another part of the country and Simon transferred to a second primary school. At this stage came what seems the classic example of a gifted child seeming to be of low ability. After one and a half terms his class teacher spoke of considerable behavioural problems. She said she would like a cage in the corner of the room to put him in.

The mother saw the Head; his opening words were, 'Don't worry, we have a remedial teacher coming in next term. She will help Simon.' After the parent expressed amazement, the Headmaster suggested that Simon be assessed by an educational psychologist.

After a long interview with Simon the psychologist reported that he was very intelligent, with an IQ around 146, and that logic was his strong point. She said he made the tests seem ridiculous.

His conversation was so mature that the educational psychologist had to remind herself constantly that she was talking to a child. He was said to show great organizational ability and egotism. He was described as a born nonconformist. It was suggested that he should be encouraged, whatever the disruption to school and family life. (The family did not take this advice and there were many collisions because of this.)

He was also said to be a perfectionist. This led to a low ability assessment at school. As he couldn't bear either to make a mistake or to admit to his ignorance, he never got very far with his work. He preferred to be labelled as the class clown, or as the naughty boy, in this way he indulged in disruptive behaviour in order to conceal his secret.

The Headmaster dealt with the situation by inventing a class/school monitor job for him – to hive off his energy into organizing things and by putting him in the top group.

The parents were haunted by the thought – for a long time – of similar children, similarly misjudged, with families who weren't articulate enough to instigate investigations at school.

Simon's parents were perceptive and articulate, but if they had not been would Simon's potential have been recognized? If his potential had not been recognized and if his teachers had not then attempted to meet some of his special needs, would his frustration and boredom have persisted and moved towards maladjustment? And were either the achievements of Simon or the representations of his parents likely to be respected by the school?

No matter what the origins are of differences between children, the basic aim of education is to provide an environment in which each child is educated according to his ability and aptitude so that as William Carlysle put it, each should become all he was created capable of being. All the rough edges to that marvellous idea are shown in the case of Simon and a thousand other Simons.

No one would deny a gifted mathematician a sophisticated education because he came from a group or a 'social class' with a low *average* IQ. The 'idealization of the average' as Edmond Holmes HMI wrote in *What is and What might Be* (1911) is of little practical use. It is the individual who counts; it is he who must learn.

Many children are crippled by their environment (as Simon could have been) and I have written earlier of the effects of bad food, poor talk and low expectation. For those who value statistics, one child in six in Britain lives in an overcrowded home; one in eleven in a house with no hot water; and one in six is part of a family where there are five or more children. Twice as many children of unskilled workers die in the first month of life as children of professional workers. Childhood can be a major time of poverty along with early married life and old age. Children still die now for nineteenth-century reasons. Life is a lottery and the effects on the *individual* of combinations of bad circumstances can be crippling. But disadvantage and its effects are complex. Poverty may cause one child to steal, another to better himself, and a third to continue poor but honest. Although over-crowding is twice as common in Scotland as in England, Scottish children are better readers. Because each child is unique in intelligence, talents and personality from the moment of concepiton, blanket treatment is no good. Some children need pushing, others need freedom. Confident, outgoing children often do well on discovery methods; shyer children often like more structured work – knowing the rules beforehand. Whatever the characteristics of the child, success needs to be found for him and his talents developed to the full. In other words, nurture is vitally important. We cannot do much about our genes except as Bernard Shaw said wryly, to choose our parents wisely.

I mentioned IQ tests at the start of this chapter. They have their uses in a rough and ready way, though they tell us little about the fine grain of the mind. It is perhaps worth quoting Binet's (1908) original notion of 'intelligence' (he after all invented the famous IQ test). It sums up the marvellous variability of people which is the strength of society:

> Our examination of intelligence cannot take account of all those qualities – attention, will, popularity, perseverance, teachableness and courage which play so important a part in school work, and also in after life; for life is not so much a conflict of intelligence as a struggle between characters.

References

BINET, A. (1908) *L'année psychologique* but quoted in *Psychological Tests of Educable Capacity* (The Hadow Report) HMSO

DEVON EDUCATION DEPARTMENT (1977) *Find the Gifted Child* Devon Education Department, County Hall, Exeter

HOLMES, E. (1911) *What is and what might be* Constable

Some suggestions to help your child

Here is a summary of some practical points the book makes that may help sound growth of mind and body.

1 During pregnancy eat a balanced diet containing plenty of fresh food, eggs, cheese, milk and meat. Both before and after birth the developing brain is hungry for protein. The brain is beginning to grow really fast in the last three months of pregnancy and in the first two years of life and this spurt may be a 'once-only' opportunity to build the brain properly. In other words *chronic* bad feeding, and especially shortage of protein during pregnancy, in the suckling period and in the first two or three years of life, can harm the intellect.

2 Don't smoke or drink spirits during pregnancy. Smoking during pregnancy may cause changes in a developing baby's blood vessels and so increase the risk of heart disease in later life. If you smoke regularly you also run the risk of having a baby with a low birth weight and who will grow to be a smaller child than average, possibly backward in intelligence. Alcohol in excess is bad for the same reasons.

3 Babies are fashioned to live on mother's milk and it is the best food by far, even up to a year, though it needs supplementing with a variety of other foods (particularly those containing iron) after about three months. The mixture of foods it contains is right and it has the bonus of protecting the baby from disease during the first few vulnerable months of life. Suckling is also an excellent method of slimming after pregnancy, of lessening the risk of getting a breast tumour in later life and of controlling the urge to batter a baby when irritated by it.

4   It is important to send a child to school with a full stomach. A decent breakfast makes the day; without it a child will lose the energy to learn by mid-morning, may become tired, listless, and unable to concentrate. Remember it can be eighteen hours between an evening meal one day and school lunch on the next.

5   Growth in height is a sensitive indicator of health and happiness. To grow well, in addition to a good mixed diet, a child needs security and a comfortable loving relationship with praise and encouragement, as well as disapproval when appropriate.

6   With adults the message is getting across that they may be able to stave off heart and lung disease by preventive measures; there is much less consciousness of the need for preventive measures for children, but childhood is a vital time to start good behaviour patterns to prevent later disease. Like adults, children should not smoke (the younger a child starts to smoke the greater are his chances of dying early), they should take enough exercise, keep on the thin side, and cut down on sugar and ordinary fats like butter and fatty meat. Substitute the softer margarines and vegetable oils like sunflower and corn oils for some of the 'hard' fats. Our health is largely in our own hands and these simple rules may help to prevent serious adult disease such as lung cancer, heart attack, stroke and diabetes. Simple cleanliness, like handwashing before eating, is a good rule, though hard to implement.

7   Accidents are the largest single cause of death in children between the ages of one and fifteen. Traffic is the most complex environment a child can experience, and road accidents which involve children who are walking, playing and cycling take a heavy toll. Most children in the nursery and primary years are scared of the road. They are biologically incapable of meeting its demands and are quite unreliable in traffic, darting out on impulse. The peak period for domestic accidents is the first five years; falls from chairs, down the stairs, and poisoning are common; burns and scalds are less common. 'Prevention' is an easy word to use. But a young child needs protection while an older child needs to be taught how to protect himself. Children should not be left on their own in traffic up to the age of seven

or eight and not on a bike until nine. Set a good example in traffic to a child because he will learn more from your behaviour than from your explanations. Teach him to walk on the pavement and to understand traffic lights. When older the Cycling Proficiency Test is valuable. Sensible home measures are necessary: fireguards; child-resistant tops to poisonous household fluids; care with tablets, medicines and domestic equipment like spin dryers and kettles. Many accidents take place when children are *alone*.

8 Tooth decay is rife. Seventy per cent of five-year-olds have some decaying teeth and over 80 per cent of eight-year-olds have one or more bad teeth. Sugar does the damage. Don't give a baby a dummy containing sweet syrup or bottles of sweet milk or juice as a comforter. They will rot his front teeth. If a child pleads for biscuit money to spend at playtime, be firm and offer fruit instead. Cut down on all sugary foods and see that he brushes his teeth twice a day under supervision up to about eight anyway. Fluoride tablets available from chemists help to give stronger teeth for children if taken up to the age of twelve or fourteen.

9 The brain at birth is a bit like a blank slate ready for the lessons of experience. Within a few days of birth a baby is learning through his eyes and ears. As he develops he focuses the spotlight of his attention on the sounds you make or on your face or on something that interests him. As he does so, what he learns is being written on the slate, and he uses what he has learned to think and speak. All the time new experiences modify the old. But the quality of the experience you give him in play and language is crucial for his thinking and reasoning.

10 Talk to your child. Don't let the brain machinery rust by not bothering or, when he is older, by giving 'shut-up' answers to his questions. Talk naturally to him, even before he can understand. Ask questions when he is older and give him time to answer. Help him all the way along the preschool and primary years to *interpret* what he sees and feels and so to stretch his small vocabulary. But do not destroy the silent pleasure he gets from looking, smelling, feeling and listening by too much interference with books and explanations.

However, he will not learn simply by the light of nature, you have got to stage-manage experiences for him to develop his language. Simply to love a child and nothing else means that he will become totally retarded in motor skills and in his capacity to talk and understand. Children of two have been found who can only grunt and know no words because their mothers neither talked nor played with them. Remember the Victorian games you grandparents played with you and use them: 'I spy with my little eye something beginning with . . .', alphabet games, memory games, drawing and writing 'consequences'.

11 The brain is finely tuned and is in a two-way dynamic relationship with the environment within days of birth and seems to develop its powers by practice. At four weeks the brain has developed far enough for a baby to detect the most salient parts of a pattern – the mother's eyes. As the brain unfolds and strengthens its powers, entire patterns can be encoded where previously only isolated elements were recorded; so now a face is smiled at not just the eyes. Talking with a baby and, when older, sharing little experiences together (for example, watching a spider spinning or a sparrow on the windowsill) helps the brain to develop language and thought. A baby will be bored if left propped up in front of a television or imprisoned in a cot or pram for long periods. For healthy brain development he needs *from birth* a great deal of active encouragement, speaking to, and contact with an adult.

12 There is much evidence that the young brain is robust and can catch up after a bad start if proper stimulation through play and talk is given. This basic resilience should encourage foster and adoptive parents.

13 The left side of the brain in most people is the side that thinks and speaks in words; the right is good at recognizing patterns like faces and is perhaps 'artistic'. Both sides work together to ensure fine balance in thought and action. Do not pamper one side of the brain at the expense of the other. The education of the head, the heart *and* the eye and hand is important for opening a child's eyes to the world. So give balanced experience – mathematical, scientific, artistic and practical – early on. None of the things you do with him would be strictly mathematical

but that does not matter. Maths and science could be involved in simple cookery or washing a doll in the basin and would take their place in play and language. Don't forget, manual skills are just as important and unique in man as his language gift. At three, cutting with blunt scissors, drawing with a fat crayon, painting with a large brush, building with bricks, should be encouraged.

14 There are slight differences in brain development in girls and boys. The left hemisphere is slightly ahead of the right in girls, the opposite in boys. Preschool girls have greater verbal facility, boys are more practical. These basic differences are reinforced by our culture. Boys of five, given time, can catch up on any linguistic deficiencies. Girls learn much about the world through talk and might miss out on practical play experiences. It is hard for them to catch up on such concrete play experiences which are the basis of maths and science. So see that both girls and boys of preschool age are involved in experiment, and give both plenty of practice in language skills.

15 Understanding brain function can help explain how a child learns to read; how the brain searches for visual clues – and clues from grammar and syntax and the context to make sense of the text. But children are naturally disposed to learn how to do it. They can only learn to read by reading. They need, of course, skilful teaching and lots of encouragement to guess at the meaning and not a strict demand for word-for-word accuracy. When your child is very young make experiences with books pleasurable. Read him stories on your knee. He will discover that something called a book is used by mother to read stories to him and that listening to a story and looking at the pictures is something enjoyable. If done regularly it will remove all risk of illiteracy later on.

16 It is a basic characteristic of the brain that its nerve cells repeat patterns of activity and it is important to know that future skills like walking, talking, eating, playing or writing are developed from these earliest patterns. Complex skills such as those mentioned can often be used again much more easily once the nerve pathways have been formed. As the brain works on repetitions it is important to *repeat* words, phrases and songs and

to encourage looking, smelling and listening by doing the same thing over and over again so that the nerve pathways become well used (a child loves repetition anyway – a favourite story or game). But it you want a child to be good with his hands and to take pleasure and interest in looking and listening it is important to link repetition with enjoyable sensations – warmth and comfort for example while listening to a story on a knee. Such associated pleasure is a strong booster to learning – to love books for instance, long before going to school.

17 A good night's sleep is important for you and your child to give the brain 'the rest it deserves' after all the activities of the day. Sleep in fact may be a time of repair and maintenance of the nerve cells used in learning and memory. Practically, 'sleeping on it' helps to clarify and consolidate what has been learned. A problem often becomes clearer after a period of 'no learning' like sleep, or after a bit of gardening, playing the piano, making a model or going for a bike ride. Start these relaxing habits early in children.

18 The 'silly' faces and noises which we are all inclined to make at a baby are important in teaching him to interpret human signs and 'signals'. Facial expression and movements develop very early. Your baby will copy yours. So encourage signs of pleasure with your pleasure and try to counter signs of grief or pain. When a bit older, play games where you can laugh *with* him at something. This is one of the strongest bonding behaviours known.

19 In 8 above I have talked about the lessons of experience inscribed on the brain. One basic experience is the need for a mother (or another loved person because the blood tie is not important) who can give a child time and patience and provide a consistent, continuing model for him. Another is the *support* of his family who need to understand what is going on at school or playgroup so that a child does not come home to a vacuum or worse to a negative influence. *Severe* family discord and disharmony may be more damaging to a child emotionally and intellectually than the separation of parents and break-up of the family.

20 School phobias may not be a straightforward fear of school.

Their cause can be insecurity at home. A child might be worried that his mother might run away or die or be lonely while he is at school. Don't enforce discipline by threatening any of these things.

21 Each and every child is unique; success needs to be found for each one of them so that each should become all that he was created capable of being. This surely is the aim of education, which parents in the home and teachers in the school are working together to achieve.

Bibliography

*BLACKIE, J. (1967) *Inside the Primary School* HMSO
*BLAKEMORE, C. (1977) *Mechanics of the Mind* Cambridge University Press
BOWLBY, J. (1973) *Separation, Anxiety and Anger* Hogarth Press
BRAIN, R. (Ed) (1960) *Mind, Perception and Science* Oxford University Press
*BRIERLEY, J. K. (1967) *Biology and the Social Crisis* Heinemann
——. (1973) *The Thinking Machine* Heinemann
*——. (1976) *The Growing Brain: Childhood's Crucial Years* NFER
*DARLINGTON, C. D. (1966) *Genetics and Man* Penguin
DHSS (1977) *Fit for the Future* (The Court Report) HMSO
ECCLES, J. I. (1965) *The Brain and the Unity of Conscious Experience* Cambridge University Press
GREENE, R. (1971) *Human Hormones* World University Library
HUTT, S. J. and HUTT, C. (Eds) (1973) *Early Human Development* Oxford University Press
*JACKSON, R. H. (Ed) (1977) *Children, the Environment and Accidents* Pitman Medical
*KAGAN, J. (1974) Man's enormous capacity to catch up *Times Educational Supplement* September
*KELLMER PRINGLE, M. (1975) *The Needs of Children* Hutchinson
*LURIA, A. R. (1973) *The Working Brain* Penguin
MARSHALL, W. A. (1968) *Development of the Brain* Oliver and Boyd
PENFIELD, W. (1975) *The Mystery of the Mind* Princeton
PIAGET, J. (1977) *The Moral Judgment of a Child* Penguin
*ROSE, S. (1976) *The Conscious Brain* Penguin
ROYAL COLLEGE OF PHYSICIANS (1977) *Smoking or Health?* Pitman Medical
RUSSELL, W. R. (1975) *Explaining the Brain* Oxford University Press
RUTTER, M. and MADGE, N. (1976) *Cycles of Disadvantage* Heinemann
*SANDELS, S. (1968) *Children in Traffic* Elek
*TANNER, J. M. (1961) *Education and Physical Growth* University of London Press
*TINBERGEN, N. (1975) The importance of being playful *Times Educational Supplement* January
* Suitable for the general reader

Index

Page numbers in italics refer to diagrams and tables

protein—*cont'd*
  in mixed diet 31–2, *33*
  intake of five-year-olds *18*
puberty 22, 26, 27–8
  induced 29

reading
  and brain hemisphere coordination
    87–8
  critical time 89
  dyslexia 88–90
reasoning 69–70, 84, 85
routine, importance of *12*

school phobia 81–2, 83, 106–7
Shaw, George Bernard 101
Shelley, Percy 91
single parents 7, 30
sleep, importance of 106
smoking
  effect on foetus 19, 42, 102
  and heart disease 37, 41–2, 103
social class
  and height 25, 34–5
  and illness 37
  and infant mortality 13–14
  and opportunity 100
spatial ability 87, 89
  sex differences 92–3, 94–5, 106
speech 48–59
  brain physiology and 51–3
  case studies 48–50

games 56, 105
mark of mankind 60
non-verbal signals 54, 56–8
optimum time for development 21,
    48–9, 92
practice makes perfect 53–9, 104–5
stimulus essential 49–50
timetable *65*
squint 21
stress, effect on growth and health 29–30
sub-normality 96–7

teachers
  coping with individuality 98–101
  influence on child 11, 70
Thompson, Flora 55
touch 62, 69
twins 26, 97

verbal intelligence 87, 89
  sex differences 92–3, 94–5, 106
vision
  development in babies 63–9
  'visual alphabet' 75, 79

weight
  birthweight, factors affecting 18, 19, 26
  overweight and heart disease 37–40
  period of fastest increase 27
welfare services 36
work as learning situation 70–2
working mothers 7